Working with Oracle GoldenGate 12c

From Implementation to Troubleshooting

Working with Oracle GoldenGate 12c

From Implementation to Troubleshooting

Gavin Powell

CRC Press
Taylor & Francis Group
Boca Raton London New York

CRC Press is an imprint of the
Taylor & Francis Group, an **informa** business

CRC Press
Taylor & Francis Group
6000 Broken Sound Parkway NW, Suite 300
Boca Raton, FL 33487-2742

First issued in paperback 2022

© 2019 by Gavin Powell
CRC Press is an imprint of Taylor & Francis Group, an Informa business

No claim to original U.S. Government works

ISBN 13: 978-1-03-247578-3 (pbk)
ISBN 13: 978-1-138-19757-2 (hbk)

DOI: 10.1201/9781315277196

Visit the Taylor & Francis Web site at
http://www.taylorandfrancis.com

and the CRC Press Web site at
http://www.crcpress.com

Dedication

For Mei Mei - Tienshing

Contents

List of Figures

List of Tables

About the Author

Gavin Powell is a veteran IT practitioner and author of a number of Oracle publications. Gavin has extensive experience in many databases, including over a decade working with Oracle databases.

Gavin has authored the following books:

- *Database Modeling: From Zero to 60 in 4 Seconds*
- *Oracle Performance Tuning for 10^9R2*
- *Oracle SQL Jumpstart with Examples (with Carol McCullough-Dieter)*
- *Oracle Data Warehouse Tuning for 10gR2*
- *Oracle High-Performance Tuning for 9i and 10g*

Introduction

The overall goal of this book is to demonstrate the basics of using GoldenGate with Oracle® Database. GoldenGate is an excellent replication tool that can be used to replicate between one or more Oracle databases, as well as other non-Oracle databases transparently. The road map for this book includes chapters covering GoldenGate architecture, installation, configuration, basic administration, loading data into a replicated GoldenGate Oracle database, and finally applying GoldenGate in various practical scenarios. The end of the book includes a chapter covering both installing and deinstalling GoldenGate as easy to follow sequences of events (Linux® only).

Chapter 1

GoldenGate Architecture

The goal of this chapter is to describe the general architecture and purpose of GoldenGate, divided up as a description of various replication methods, followed by detailed internal architecture, including various processes, checkpoints, extract trails, groupings, internal change sequencing, and globalization.

1.1 Different Replication Methods

Replication in computer science is the process of duplicating both information and active change on that information. This process can occur in one direction, in both directions, between two computers, or even between many computers. Oracle Corporation likes to label each one of these architectural structures (called *topologies*) with distinctive names, where each of these topologies has a very specific application function:

- **Unidirectional.** Replication occurs from a source to a target machine in one (uni) direction (master to slave). This creates a constantly maintained copy of a source database, replicating typically to a reporting database or standby (failover) database, where no changes can be made on the target.
- **Broadcast.** Classic replication is where a database is distributed from a single source to two or more targets (master to slave). This topology is somewhat of a dated approach. Its purpose is to spread source database information to multiple locations in order to improve access times to information by localizing data. With the advent of extensive broadband network installations, this topology has become less important to individual companies; however, it has become useful for cloud services such as Amazon Web Services, but at the server and not the database level.
- **Consolidation.** The opposite of broadcast where multiple sources are consolidated into one target (master to slave), such as in a data warehouse or data mart (a data mart is a subset of a data warehouse). Data warehouses tend to gather and reprocess information from disparate sources, and mold it into a data set that can be used to predict patterns and trends.
- **Cascading.** Allows for dividing up databases into multiple layers of source and target environments (master to slave), with the purpose of allowing for performant scalability.
- **Bi-Directional.** Used for standby or automated real-time failover environments in order to help cater to high-availability applications. If a source database fails, then the target database automatically takes over servicing the end user population, and preferably instantaneously. This topology can allow for changes on the target without disrupting the information on the source. This structure is

a master-to-master form of replication, where all information and change is replicated from both source *to* target, to both source *and* target.

- **Peer-to-Peer.** This topology is used to provide for high availability in the form of connecting multiple databases into an inter-connected, inter-related, concurrently available processing environment. All information and change is replicated from all sources to all targets (and visa versa), constantly and simultaneously. This is a master-to-master replicating system that creates a form of a clustered or grid connected environment.

1.1.1 Master-to-Slave Replication

Master-to-slave replication, as shown in Figure 1.1, means that information and changes to that information are passed from a source database to a target database; however, information is never passed back from target to source, and nothing can be changed on the slave database. All changes originate on the source database, but some database engines would allow new additions into the target as long as they don't conflict with anything from the source. Also, database changes are divided up into two different categories: (1) Data Manipulation Language (DML) that changes data in tables, and (2) Data Definition Language (DDL) that changes tables and other metadata objects (data about the data). With respect to replication, not all database engines and configurations will support DDL changes, where DDL changes might have to be replicated manually.

1.1.2 Master-to-Master Replication

Master-to-master replication, as shown in Figure 1.2, is extremely complex, in that its objective is to replicate information between two or more

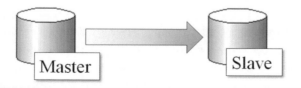

Figure 1.1   Master-to-Slave Replication Duplicates Change from One Database to Another

databases, to all the other databases in the group, regardless of in which database a change is made. Master-to-master replication copies information from all servers to all other servers, where each is both source and target.

Figure 1.2   Master-to-Master Replication Duplicates Change from All Databases to All Other Databases

1.1.3 GoldenGate Options for Use with Oracle® Database

These options are already covered previously in this chapter but are worth mentioning again from the perspective of the application of the architecture, as opposed to the architecture itself:

- **Unidirectional.** A reporting database
- **Broadcast.** Single direction replication that distributes the same information geographically
- **Consolidation.** Aggregate data from multiple sources into data warehouses, data marts, and BigData databases
- **Cascading.** Scales up a system into multiple layers
- **Bi-Directional.** Implements standby (failover) databases
- **Peer-to-Peer.** Clustered or grid database for high availability

1.2 The Architecture of GoldenGate

Like many other parts of Oracle software, GoldenGate consists of a structure that encompasses a number of appropriately named locations, in addition to named processes that connect those locations. The basic structure is two databases, consisting of a source and target database, plus extract files that contain the sequence of DML and DDL changes from the source database, to be applied to the target database through replication files located on the target server. Figure 1.3 shows a general picture of the architecture of Oracle GoldenGate software.

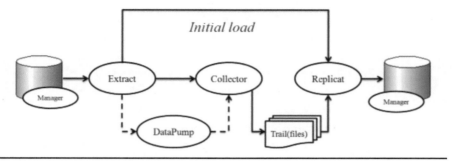

Figure 1.3   The Internal Architecture of Oracle GoldenGate Software

1.2.1 The Manager Process

The Manager process controls GoldenGate and must be up and running on all databases to allow for the Extract and Replicat processes to be started up. The Manager process starts and stops GoldenGate processing, any dynamic processes, assigns port number allocations, purging of trail files, as well as managing reporting.

1.2.2 The Extract Process

The Extract process captures changes from a source database and usually runs on the source database but can run on a target database as well. The Extract process can be used to run initial loads from a single set of source tables between source and target databases. After the initial load, the Extract process is used to synchronize (replicate) DML and DDL changes between source and target databases on an ongoing basis, by using logs of change to replicate (copy) changes from sources to targets, duplicating the sequence of changes on target environments. There are some important points to note:

- Commit and rollback of change is part of the normal transactional logging sequence of a database and will simply be duplicated to target databases as it occurs on the source. This replication of persisted change is achieved simply by writing committed changes to trails, where a rollback would undo changes before a commit occurred. So commits are persisted to the trail and rollbacks are not, because rollbacks are not needed.

> *Rollbacks are part of transactional logs in a standard transactional database, because the fastest approach is to write all changes to a database, and then reverse those changes in the event of a rollback, regardless of when a commit is executed. The assumption is that commits are far more frequent than rollbacks, and thus duplication of activity is sacrificed to cater to overall performance.*

- Source and target databases can be explicitly configured where not all objects (such as tables) on a source database are to be replicated to target databases. The Extract process will simply not replicate changes to objects that are not configured to replicate (excluded from replication configuration).
- Replication can be performed in parallel using multiple matching sets of parallel executed Extract processes, Replicat processes, and extraction (persistence) trails.
- Online Extract and Replicat processes run until stopped by a user, continuously extracting and replicating DDL and DML changes occurring on the source, to the target.

> *The EXTRACT and REPLICAT parameters help to configure Extract and Replicat processing.*

1.2.3 The Replicat Process

The Replicat process essentially executes the replication (or repetition) of DML and DDL processing as executed on the source and copied into the trails, where those same trails are subsequently used to provide DML and DDL change feed information into the target database. Replicat is used to execute what are called *initial loads* (loading a database from scratch), as well as to apply changes that synchronize between source and target databases; this is called *change synchronization* (syncing changes between source and target to cause the target to be synchronized with the source). Some points to remember:

- Replicat can be configured in coordinated or integrated modes, where integrated mode applies to Oracle databases, and coordinated mode can be used to coordinate between Oracle and some other type of target database environment.
- Replicat can have a delay configured to allow for a delay of erroneous application using a parameter called the DEFERAPPLYINTERVAL parameter.
- Further information on GoldenGate parameters can be found in the online Oracle GoldenGate documentation on Oracle's website, at docs.oracle.com.
- An initial load of a target replication database can be executed using a special run of the Replicat process, where there are known starting and ending points in time for the replication. The SPECIALRUN parameter can be configured in this case in order to allow for reading between two points of the Extract process trails.

See the video "Finding, Downloading, and Navigating Oracle GoldenGate Documentation" at www.ezoracle tutor.com.

1.2.4 The Collector Process

The Collector process runs on the target database, writing changes from the source database into the trail files, to be consumed by the Replicat process on the target database.

1.2.5 Checkpoints

A checkpoint in a database environment is a set of pointers that describe the state of a database at a specific juncture (point in time), and that checkpoint is stored so that the checkpoint can be reverted to if necessary. A recovery back to a previous checkpoint places a database into the state of change it was in at the juncture of the checkpoint. So the failure of any of the parts between a constantly synchronizing (extracting) source, and a constantly (replicating) target database, can be recovered back to a previous checkpoint juncture (a previous point in time).

In reality, GoldenGate only has to re-read the transaction logs on the source database in order to recover to a checkpoint. Checkpoints are a part of the target database in GoldenGate and are stored by the Replicat process on the target database as a table called the *checkpoint table.* So GoldenGate checkpoints themselves are stored as part of backup processing on the target database, which is more secure in maintaining recoverability. Checkpoint information stored includes read and write details, what is captured by the Extract process, and what is applied by the Replicat process. It is, however, important to note that checkpoints are not transactional based with respect to a DML change on the source database, and thus a checkpoint can be created within a database change transaction, and controlled by a time interval using a GoldenGate configuration parameter called CHECKPOINTSECS. So when database backups are performed for source and target GoldenGate databases, one should also include the GoldenGate trail files, given that the trails are not stored inside source or target databases.

1.2.6 Extract Files

In general, GoldenGate can perform different types of extraction depending on the phase of implementation, where (1) an initial load takes an initial consistent snapshot of the source for an initialization loading into the target; (2) continuously updating is later performed by applying DML and DDL changes from source to target, in the sequence in which those changes have already been applied to the source database; and (3) initial loads and continuous replication can be sent outside of an Oracle database to a target database other than Oracle.

As shown in Figure 1.3, the trail files are a file system stored sequence of transactions produced after the Extract process (the Collector process). Those trails are in turn read as a record of committed source database transactions, as a way to form an architecture in the replication process that: (1) allows for recoverability outside of the source and target environments; and (2) allows the Extract and Replicat processes to execute without being dependent upon each other—failure on one server will not cause failure on others, which is important for a replication tool that can also function as a failover. The trail can be located on the source (Extract or Local Trail) or target (Remote Trail) database server, and even on another server in between (Remote Trail), or any combination thereof. The Extract Trail can even be stored as an Extract File (one or more recycling files), where checkpoints do not exist (Extract and Remote Trails do record checkpoints). Extract processes must each be linked to a trail into which committed transactions can be generated, which must be unique if local (on the source server). When using data pump processes to write trails, there should be one trail for each data pump, and those trails can even have the same name, as long as those trails are located on separate remote servers.

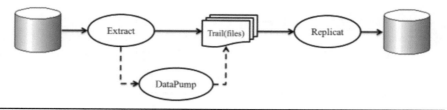

Figure 1.4   GoldenGate Internal Architecture and Trails

As shown in Figure 1.4, the trail can be located on either server (or both) and even be accessed by data pump processing, which extracts DDL and DML from a local trail where changes are moved to another trail that would be read by the Replicat process.

Data Pump

Data pump is Oracle Database technology used primarily for making consistent, *re-playable* DDL and DML export dumps from an Oracle database. Data pump can also be used to perform a small amount of expression-based data and object filtering (copy only specific objects or data items), data mapping (change the names of objects and data structures), as well as data conversion (transform data between different formats) during the export data pumping process. So data pump can be used to pump data from one server to another, much like data warehousing Extract Transport and Load (ETL) processing.

> *Expression-based processing is functional based where one value is passed in and another single value is passed out, as in x = (y+1), where substituting y=3 results in x=4; the point is that a single value is returned so that the expression (x+1) can be embedded inside a Structured Query Language (SQL) coded query.*

Data pump can also be configured in pass-through mode, where no ETL data manipulations occur. Data pump processing is effectively an additional Extract process and runs on the source database and writes to the trail on the source database server, as shown in Figure 1.5.

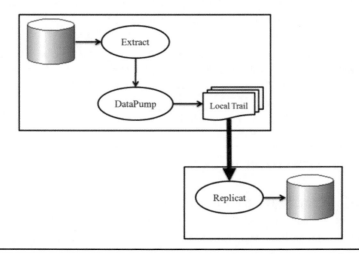

Figure 1.5 Data Pump Runs on Source into a Local Trail

When not using data pump, then the Extract process that runs on a source server database must send extracted committed transactions to the trail (file or files), which must be running on a remote trail. The remote trail is running on the target, which is another server that protects from failure, as shown in Figure 1.6.

Data pump allows for the effective further isolation between source and target databases in order to allow for easier recovery from failure without disconnecting the source and target systems. Data pump builds another layer, in that it allows for both consolidation (many sources to one target such as in a data warehouse) and distribution (one source to many targets that distribute data as in large cloud service providers). The further isolation between source and target inherently provides the following:

- Insurance against network failure.
- Insurance for failure at one or more targets.
- ETL processing capabilities within replication processing helping to limit processing time further down the processing chain of events.

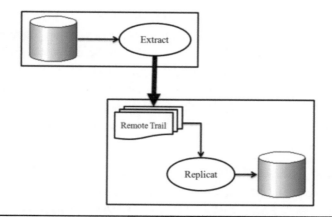

Figure 1.6   GoldenGate Extract Trail Must Be a Remote Trail if Data Pump Is Not Used

- Consolidation into a single data warehouse target should not be halted by the failure of one of many sources, where the data pump processing occurs on the sources. Warehouse processing is not dependent upon committed transaction trails that are generated on one specific source database server.
- Multiple targets can be serviced by multiple data pump Extract processes running on a single source database server, and thus network failure to a single target server does not affect all target servers at once.

1.2.7 Groups

Processing groups are used to describe and create multiple sets of related Extract or Replicat processes, where each group runs in parallel to other groups. So a group can contain a process such as an Extract or a Replicat process, along with configuration parameter files, trails, and checkpoints (Replicat). The ADD EXTRACT and ADD REPLICAT commands are used to create groups in the GoldenGate Software Command Line Interface (GGSCI); GGSCI is the GoldenGate character-based shell interface.

1.2.8 The Commit Sequence Number (CSN)

A GoldenGate CSN is used to identify GoldenGate replicated transactions, which are used to ensure data integrity (consistency) on target databases by identifying the juncture of a committed transaction. The CSN can be used to link between where to place the Extract process in the transaction log on the source database, and the Replicat process in the trails on the target database. So a CSN identifies the point in time at which a transaction is committed on the target replicated database by the Replicat process. The CSN can be useful in placing the Extract process at a specific juncture in the sequence of transactions, or also to place the Replicat process on the trail.

Oracle and DB2 have variable-length CSNs. Oracle depends on Oracle System Change Numbers (SCNs), whereas other databases generally have fixed length CSNs.

1.2.9 Support for Globalized Character Sets

GoldenGate allows for replication between source and target databases using what is called *native language encoding,* based on the character sets of those source and target databases. In other words, character-based content is replicated by GoldenGate between differing character sets; the detailed mechanics of this process is out of the scope of this book. A very useful online posting on this topic can be found here:

```
jinyuwang.weebly.com/core-platform/oracle-goldengate-
globalization
```

1.3 So What's Next?

As a first chapter in a book introducing Oracle GoldenGate, it is important to get an overall non-detailed picture of how GoldenGate works as a piece of replication software. Thus, this chapter briefly describes the general architecture of GoldenGate, including all the pieces, what they do, and how they all fit together to make a whole. The next chapter covers installing and basic configuration of GoldenGate within source and target Oracle databases.

Chapter 2

Installing GoldenGate

The goal of this chapter is to demonstrate installation of GoldenGate software, as well as some basic required logging configuration that must be added to source and target Oracle® databases. Also included are pre-installation steps, downloading software, and Oracle connectivity.

2.1 Pre-Installation Steps

GoldenGate is just another piece of software in some respects, and as with any piece of software, it has certain requirements before installing. For example, one would not want to try to install the Windows® operating system onto an Apple Mac computer; thus the requirement of needing a Windows-compatible computer is a prerequisite or pre-installation step.

At the time of writing this book, the basic system-level requirements for GoldenGate were found at this URL:

```
http://www.oracle.com/technetwork/middleware/ias/downloads/
fusion-certification-100350.html
```

The Oracle GoldenGate manuals can be found at http://docs.oracle.com/golengate/c1221/gg-winux/index.html

---

The servers used to write this book are two 64-bit Dell servers containing Oracle Linux (Red Hat 5), with 8Gb of Random Access Memory (RAM) and a terabyte (Tb) of disk space each. Installing software generally requires super-user or administration-type privileges for installing, which implies root for Linux® or UNIX®, and Administrator for Windows. The graphical Oracle Universal Installer (OUI) is an Oracle built in Java® application and can be used to install GoldenGate; there is also a character-based interface that will not be used in this book.

GoldenGate obviously requires two databases, given that GoldenGate is primarily a replication tool, where a source database replicates or duplicates information, and its operations are replicated to at least one other target database. The two databases should be properly installed, able to communicate with each other in both directions using Oracle's Transparent Network Substrate (TNS), and must both be in archivelog mode because GoldenGate replicates using log entries in various modes.

Some of the more exotic data types can cause problems for replication and possibly not be *replicatable* at all. Some datatypes can impose restrictions on available replication modes—see the following URL to understand what is and is not allowed:

```
https://docs.oracle.com/goldengate/1212/gg-winux/GIORA/
system_requirements.htm
```

2.2 Downloading and Installing

Downloading is usually very simple, but there has been a lot of software available from Oracle Corporation in recent times, and it can be tough to navigate through the clutter; the process begins with downloading.

2.2.1 Downloading GoldenGate Software

Acquiring and downloading GoldenGate is free (licensing is not), and the easiest way to get the software is by using the following steps:

- www.oracle.com
- Rollover (move the mouse over) the Downloads link and click See All under the Middleware section, as shown in Figure 2.1.
- The GoldenGate link is under Middleware on the next page—click it!

Figure 2.1   Finding the GoldenGate Software Download

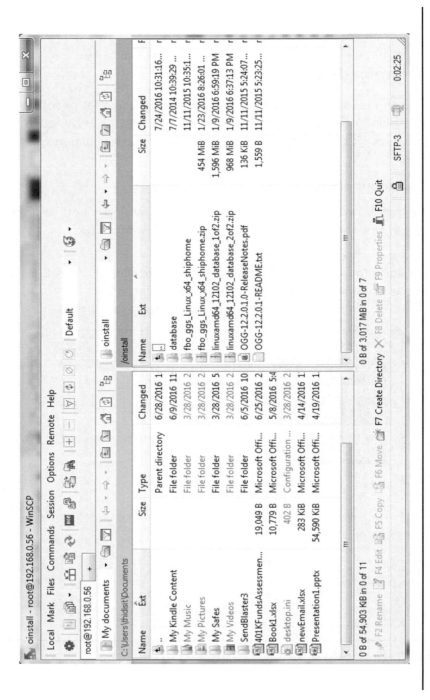

Figure 2.2 Moving GoldenGate Software to a Server

- Click the Accept License Agreement radio button at the top of the page.
- The version selected for this book is the Linux 64-bit version of Oracle GoldenGate, titled Oracle GoldenGate V12.2.0.1.1 for Oracle on Linux x86-64.
- At this stage a login may be forced; if an account is not already available, then do create a free account.
- At the end of the process, a prompt to download a zip file will be encountered; select to download. The file will be called something like fbo_ggs_Linux_x64_shiphome.zip. Ship the downloaded file onto a server (if used) and into a path that it can be installed from as the Oracle Database super-user, such as the oracle Linux user in Linux, as shown in Figure 2.2.

2.2.2 Installing GoldenGate Software

Begin the installation process by extracting the zip file on both source and target servers, which in Linux uses the unzip command as follows:

```
unzip fbo_ggs_Linux_x64_shiphome.zip
```

Once the zip file is unzipped, check that the ORACLE_HOME and ORACLE_SID variables are set on a source server something like this:

```
[oracle@bigdata oinstall-bigdata]$ set | grep ORACLE
ORACLE_HOME=/u01/app/oracle/product/12.1.0/dbhome_1
ORACLE_SID=bigdata
```

And on a target server:

```
[oracle@failover oinstall-failover]$ set | grep ORACLE
ORACLE_HOME=/u01/app/oracle/product/12.1.0/dbhome_1
ORACLE_SID=failover
```

Next add the GoldenGate requirements to the .bash_profile, as in the example .bash_profile shown in Figure 2.3, which includes lines that are added for GoldenGate.

The next step is to run the Oracle Universal Installer (OUI) tool runInstaller for GoldenGate. You will need to execute it in X Windows either

```
if [ -f ~/.bashrc ]; then
    . ~/.bashrc
fi

umask 022

export PATH=$PATH:$HOME:/bin:/bin:/usr/bin:/usr/local/bin:/etc::/usr/sbin

export ORACLE_BASE=/u01/app/oracle
export ORACLE_HOME=$ORACLE_BASE/product/12.1.0/dbhome_1
export ORACLE_GG=$ORACLE_BASE/product/12.1.0/oggcore_1
export ORACLE_SID=bigdata
export LD_LIBRARY_PATH=$ORACLE_HOME/lib
export LD_LIBRARY_PATH=$LD_LIBRARY_PATH:$ORACLE_GG
export TNS_ADMIN=$ORACLE_HOME/network/admin
export TRACE=$ORACLE_BASE/diag/rdbms/$ORACLE_SID/$ORACLE_SID/trace
export PATH=$PATH:$ORACLE_BASE:$ORACLE_HOME:$ORACLE_HOME/bin:$TNS_ADMIN:$ORACLE_HOME/Opatch
export PATH=$PATH:$ORACLE_GG
export TMP=/tmp
export BACKUPS=/u02/app/oracle/backups

PS1="[\u@\H \W-`echo $ORACLE_SID`]\$ "

export HOST=`hostname -s`

alias rm='rm -i'
alias base='cd $ORACLE_BASE'
alias home='cd $ORACLE_HOME'
alias gghome='cd $ORACLE_GG'
alias alert='cd $TRACE'
alias lsnrlog='cd $ORACLE_BASE/diag/tnslsnr/$HOST/listener/trace'
alias tns='cd $TNS_ADMIN'
alias sqlnetlog='cd $ORACLE_HOME/network/log'
alias sqlnettrc='cd $ORACLE_HOME/network/trace'
alias dbs='cd $ORACLE_HOME/dbs'
alias backups='cd $BACKUPS'
```

Figure 2.3   Linux .bash_profile for Oracle Database with GoldenGate Added

directly on your server with an attached and appropriate screen, or using terminal emulation, such as Virtual Network Computing (VNC); the following link can help you to get VNC working:

```
http://www.oracletroubleshooter.com/using-vncserver
```

For most *nix commands, you can find the long format name of the command using the man page for that command in the operating system. Type man vncserver into a Linux shell to find that VNC is an acronym for Virtual Network Computing.

The unzipped GoldenGate download file should have been decompressed into a subdirectory, such as the following:

```
[oracle@bigdata.localdomain Disk1-bigdata]$ pwd
/oinstall/fbo_ggs_Linux_x64_shiphome/Disk1
[oracle@bigdata.localdomain Disk1-bigdata]$ ls
install  response  runInstaller  stage
```

So now cd (Change Directory) into the subdirectory and run the installer connected first as root and then as the oracle Linux user:

```
xhost +
su - oracle
cd /oinstall/fbo_ggs_Linux_x64_shiphome/Disk1
. runInstaller
```

The trail of graphics takes you through an easy-to-understand, step-by-step process. Remember to do the following:

- Select Oracle 12c.
- Pick the correct GoldenGate home (see Figure 2.3)—the installer might select the Oracle Database home, which is incorrect.
- Don't forget that there is a software (GoldenGate) and a database location, which are two separate things. The OUI will create the new directory if not already done so manually.
- Click various Next, Install, and Finish buttons at obvious junctures.

- Don't forget to run the OUI tool in the same way on both the source and the target servers.

See the video "Installing Oracle GoldenGate with the OUI":
www.ezoracletutor.com

Remember, there is also what is called a *silent installation* (command line in a shell) available for Oracle GoldenGate, but it is more complex and harder to use. You can find information on that installation in the Oracle manuals.

2.2.3 Testing GoldenGate Software

Test the GoldenGate command utility GGSCI on all source and target servers:

```
cd $ORACLE_GG
ggsci
```

The result should look like that below, where the necessary working directories can be subsequently verified, as well as created on both source and target server installations:

```
GGSCI (bigdata.localdomain) 1> create subdirs
Creating subdirectories under current diréctory /u01/app/
oracle/product/12.1.0/oggcore_1

Parameter files               /u01/app/oracle/
product/12.1.0/oggcore_1/dirprm: already exists
Report files                  /u01/app/oracle/
product/12.1.0/oggcore_1/dirrpt: already exists
Checkpoint files              /u01/app/oracle/
product/12.1.0/oggcore_1/dirchk: already exists
Process status files          /u01/app/oracle/
product/12.1.0/oggcore_1/dirpcs: already exists
SQL script files              /u01/app/oracle/
product/12.1.0/oggcore_1/dirsql: already exists
Database definitions files    /u01/app/oracle/
product/12.1.0/oggcore_1/dirdef: already exists
```

```
Extract data files              /u01/app/oracle/
product/12.1.0/oggcore_1/dirdat: already exists
Temporary files                 /u01/app/oracle/
product/12.1.0/oggcore_1/dirtmp: already exists
Credential store files          /u01/app/oracle/
product/12.1.0/oggcore_1/dircrd: already exists
Masterkey wallet files          /u01/app/oracle/
product/12.1.0/oggcore_1/dirwlt: already exists
Dump files                      /u01/app/oracle/
product/12.1.0/oggcore_1/dirdmp: already exists
GGSCI (bigdata.localdomain) 2>
```

There are many commands available in the GGSCI tool, which can be accessed using the HELP command inside GGSCI, as shown in Figure 2.4 (on next page).

2.3 Setting up Oracle Database for GoldenGate

Thus far in this chapter, only the GoldenGate software has been installed, and there is still much more to do. The next step in using GoldenGate is to configure the software and make it work, beginning with the Oracle Database networking layer.

2.3.1 Oracle Transparent Network Substrate (TNS)

The first point is to establish the Oracle TNS connection between both a source and a target database. On both servers, there needs to be connectivity to both the source and the target database by changing the tnsnames.ora file on each server. Begin by adding the IP address plus host name value pairs into the /etc/hosts files on each server, assuming IP addresses are not used in the Oracle software's tnsnames.ora files:

```
# Do not remove the following line, or various programs
# that require network functionality will fail.
127.0.0.1       localhost.localdomain   localhost     bigdata
::1 localhost.localdomain localhost6    localhost     bigdata
10.29.102.156  bigdata.localdomain      bigdata
10.29.102.158  failover.localdomain     failover
```

```
GGSCI Command Summary:

Object:           Command:
SUBDIRS           CREATE
DATASTORE         ALTER, CREATE, DELETE, INFO, REPAIR
ER                INFO, KILL, LAG, SEND, STATUS, START, STATS, STOP
EXTRACT           ADD, ALTER, CLEANUP, DELETE, INFO, KILL,
                  LAG, REGISTER, SEND, START, STATS, STATUS, STOP
                  UNREGISTER
EXTTRAIL          ADD, ALTER, DELETE, INFO
GGSEVT            VIEW
JAGENT            INFO, START, STATUS, STOP
MANAGER           INFO, SEND, START, STOP, STATUS
MARKER            INFO
PARAMETERS        EDIT, VIEW, SET EDITOR, INFO, GETPARAMINFO
REPLICAT          ADD, ALTER, CLEANUP, DELETE, INFO, KILL, LAG, REGISTER, SEND,
                  START, STATS, STATUS, STOP, SYNCHRONIZE, UNREGISTER
REPORT            VIEW
RMTTRAIL          ADD, ALTER, DELETE, INFO
TRACETABLE        ADD, DELETE, INFO
TRANDATA          ADD, DELETE, INFO
SCHEMATRANDATA    ADD, DELETE, INFO
CHECKPOINTTABLE   ADD, DELETE, CLEANUP, INFO, UPGRADE
WALLET            CREATE, OPEN, PURGE
MASTERKEY         ADD, INFO, RENEW, DELETE, UNDELETE
CREDENTIALSTORE   ADD, ALTER, INFO, DELETE
HEARTBEATTABLE    ADD, DELETE, ALTER, INFO
HEARTBEATENTRY    DELETE

Commands without an object:
(Database)        DBLOGIN, LIST TABLES, ENCRYPT PASSWORD, FLUSH SEQUENCE
                  MININGDBLOGIN, SET NAMECCSID
(DDL)             DUMPDDL
(Miscellaneous)    ! ,ALLOWNESTED | NOALLOWNESTED, CREATE SUBDIRS,
                  DEFAULTJOURNAL, FC, HELP, HISTORY, INFO ALL, OBEY, SHELL,
                  SHOW, VERSIONS, VIEW GGSEVT, VIEW REPORT
                  (note: type the word COMMAND after the ! to display the
                  ! help topic, for example: GGSCI (sys1)> help ! command

For help on a specific command, type HELP <command> <object>.

Example: HELP ADD REPLICAT
```

Figure 2.4 Inside GGSCI, Type HELP to Show All Options Under the GGSCI Command Summary

And change the $ORACLE_HOME/network/admin/tnsnames.ora files on both servers to allow the source and the target to communicate with each other through TNS at the Oracle software layer:

```
LISTENER_BIGDATA =
   (ADDRESS = (PROTOCOL = TCP)(HOST = bigdata.localdomain)
   (PORT = 1742))


BIGDATA =
```

```
(DESCRIPTION =
  (ADDRESS = (PROTOCOL = TCP)(HOST = bigdata.localdomain)
  (PORT = 1742))
  (CONNECT_DATA = (SERVER = DEDICATED) (SERVICE_NAME =
  bigdata))
)

FAILOVER =
  (DESCRIPTION =
  (ADDRESS = (PROTOCOL = TCP)(HOST = failover.
  localdomain)(PORT = 1863))
  (CONNECT_DATA = (SERVER = DEDICATED) (SERVICE_NAME =
  failover))
)
```

The registered listener is different for the target server:

```
LISTENER_FAILOVER =
  (ADDRESS = (PROTOCOL = TCP)(HOST = failover.localdomain)
  (PORT = 1863))
```

At this stage both servers should be *tnsping'able* from both as below:

```
[oracle@bigdata.localdomain dbs-bigdata]$ tnsping failover

TNS Ping Utility for Linux: Version 12.1.0.2.0 -
Production on 04-SEP-2016 12:04:17

Copyright (c) 1997, 2014, Oracle.  All rights reserved.

Used parameter files:
/u01/app/oracle/product/12.1.0/dbhome_1/network/admin/
sqlnet.ora

Used TNSNAMES adapter to resolve the alias
Attempting to contact (DESCRIPTION = (ADDRESS = (PROTOCOL =
TCP)(HOST = failover.localdomain)(PORT = 1863)) (CONNECT_
DATA = (SERVER = DEDICATED) (SERVICE_NAME = failover)))
OK (0 msec)
```

> *Extract and Replicat process parameter files can be used to encrypt usernames and passwords for connections between source and target database.*

2.3.2 Replication Logging

Oracle Database redo logs store changes to metadata, such as a table creation in the form of a CREATE TABLE command. DML commands are stored as efficiently as possible, where INSERT stores the INSERT data only, UPDATE stores the changed column value and row address only, and DELETE stores the address of the deleted row only. Redo log change vectors are stored to be as efficient as possible, but only to be *replayable* back into a source database in order to recover that failed source database, and to bring that failed Oracle Database back to a desired state and point in time again. The trouble with change vectors when replicating is that the information stored to recover a source database is not enough information when replicating to a different database. For example, a DELETE command needs more than the source database internal logical row address in order to find a row to be deleted—it needs the filter to delete that row in addition to the table name—internal logical addressing values are different between source and target databases. In reality, replication needs the entire DELETE command DML statement so that the DELETE transaction can be replicated from a source to a target database without having to refer to the source database as the task is performed. Oracle calls this extra logging *supplemental logging,* meaning that more information is generated into the Oracle source database redo logs to enable replication to a target database, and it comes in three flavors:

- **Database-level supplemental logging.** Mandatory and essentially adds supplemental logging to Oracle database redo logs. Forces all transactions to be logged and adds row chaining information.
- **Schema-level supplemental logging.** Configured inside Golden-Gate software with a number of options:
  - Additionally logs all primary key and valid unique indexes for all tables in a schema, but DDL replication is not supported. This is the minimum required for schema-level logging, maintaining uniqueness of values that are required to be unique, and using the ADD

SCHEMATRANDATA GGSCI command with the NOSCHEDULINGCOLS option (non-integrated Replicat only).

o Additionally logs primary key, unique key, and foreign key (referential integrity) information, meaning that all keys and values are logged and DDL is supported, which allows generation of all key values inside the target. This is the default setting and uses the ADD SCHEMATRANDATA GGSCI command.

o Additionally logs all columns in all tables in a schema, regardless of whether a column value is changed or is not in a transaction, using the ADD SCHEMATRANDATA GGSCI command with the ALLCOLS option.

Replication allows selection of the level of detail to be replicated, such as an entire database, or one or more specific schemas, or even as specific as one or more tables within specific schemas within a database.

• **Table-level supplemental logging.** Configured inside GoldenGate software with the same options as schema-level logging, but with the very simple difference that one can replicate table by table as opposed to schema by schema, implying that one could replicate a single schema in a database, but also a single table or a group of tables.

Database-Level Supplemental Logging

Redo logs in Oracle Database allow for transactional consistency and real-time recoverability in the case of local failure. It is important to note that when writing data to a table in an Oracle Database, the redo logs are the most important written record and are thus always written to first, storing each and every change to the database as reusable or *replayable* change vectors of transactions. Check first that archive logging is enabled in source and target databases in SQLPLUS:

```
ARCHIVE LOG LIST;
```

If the result shown is "No Archive Mode":

```
sqlplus / as sysdba
SQL> archive log list;
Database log mode              No Archive Mode
Automatic archival             Disabled
Archive destination            USE_DB_RECOVERY_FILE_DEST
Oldest online log sequence     206
Current log sequence           208
SQL>
```

then enable archive logging using the following commands:

```
SHUTDOWN IMMEDIATE;
STARTUP MOUNT;
ALTER DATABASE ARCHIVELOG;
ALTER DATABASE OPEN;
```

Supplemental logging can be configured on both source and target, depending on the configuration of GoldenGate:

```
SQL> SELECT supplemental_log_data_min, force_logging FROM
v$database;

SUPPLEME FORCE_LOGGING
-------- ---------------------------------------
NO       NO
```

If supplemental or forced logging is not implemented (set to NO as above and not YES), then change as below:

```
ALTER DATABASE ADD SUPPLEMENTAL LOG DATA;
ALTER DATABASE FORCE LOGGING;
```

Forced logging ensures that all changes are written to redo logs. Note that supplemental logging is only needed on the source, but it's prudent to configure on source and target databases. Now verify at least one log file switch on both source and target just in case:

```
ALTER SYSTEM SWITCH LOGFILE;
```

Using Flashback

Oracle allows replication of specialized data types by use of flashback technology, which allows an object to be flashed backwards to a point in time in
the past by reading both data and rollback spaces (records of recently non-
committed transactions). Specialized Oracle Database data types include
user-defined datatypes, nested tables, and XMLType datatypes. Further
details can be found on flashback at the following URL:

```
https://docs.oracle.com/goldengate/1212/gg-winux/GIORA/
setup.htm#GIORA374
```

Set the size of the amount of undo (rollback) information retained to
allow for larger transactions (on source and target):

```
ALTER SYSTEM SET UNDO_RETENTION=86400 SCOPE=BOTH;
```

The STREAMS_POOL_SIZE Parameter

Even though Oracle Database automates low-level memory parameters
such as the streams pool, current GoldenGate documentation denotes
that the streams pool parameter requires 1GB plus an extra 25% for each
extract process:

```
ALTER SYSTEM SET STREAMS_POOL_SIZE=1280M SCOPE=BOTH;
```

> *Many online sources cite disabling the recycle bin for
> GoldenGate, but this does not apply to Oracle11g and
> beyond.*

Schema-level Supplemental Logging

Where database-level supplemental logging allows replication of an entire
database, schema-level logging will enable replication of specific schemas,
such as a single application schema. In reality, one does not have to replicate an entire database—schema-level replication can be a more efficient
option, and even less intrusive and complicated. The first thing needed is

a GoldenGate schema owner on the source database that supports replication of DDL—make these changes in Oracle using SQLPLUS for both source and target:

```
CREATE BIGFILE TABLESPACE ggate
      DATAFILE '/u02/app/oracle/oradata/bigdata/ggate01.
      dbf' SIZE 1G AUTOEXTEND ON;
CREATE USER ggate IDENTIFIED BY ggate
      DEFAULT TABLESPACE ggate TEMPORARY TABLESPACE TEMP;
GRANT DBA, CONNECT, RESOURCE, UNLIMITED TABLESPACE TO ggate;
GRANT EXECUTE ON UTL_FILE TO ggate;
GRANT FLASHBACK ANY TABLE TO ggate;
```

Add a similar user to the target database as follows, where one could use the same username on both source and target, but for the purposes of avoiding confusion, separate names are used in this book:

```
CREATE BIGFILE TABLESPACE ggate
      DATAFILE '/u02/app/oracle/oradata/failover/ggate01.
      dbf' SIZE 1G AUTOEXTEND ON;
CREATE USER ggate IDENTIFIED BY ggate
      DEFAULT TABLESPACE ggate TEMPORARY TABLESPACE TEMP;
GRANT DBA, CONNECT, RESOURCE, UNLIMITED TABLESPACE TO
ggate;
GRANT EXECUTE ON UTL_FILE TO ggate;
GRANT FLASHBACK ANY TABLE TO ggate;
```

Enable GoldenGate Configuration Parameter

There is a parameter new to Oracle12c that applies to both the capture (Extract on the source) as well as the apply (Replicat on the target) servers:

```
ALTER SYSTEM SET enable_goldengate_replication=true
SCOPE=both;
```

If the above parameter is not set, then the following commands:

```
cd $ORACLE_GG
ggsci
```

```
DBLOGIN USERID ggate, PASSWORD ggate
ADD SCHEMATRANDATA email
```

may produce the following errors:

```
GGSCI (bigdata.localdomain as ggate@bigdata) 2> ADD
SCHEMATRANDATA email
ERROR: Operation not supported because enable_goldengate_
replication is not set to true.
```

The next step is to execute the GGSCI on the source database server, logging in with the DBLOGIN command using the alias of a user with the privilege of enabling schema-level supplemental logging:

```
[oracle@bigdata.localdomain ~-bigdata]$ $ORACLE_GG/ggsci

Oracle GoldenGate Command Interpreter for Oracle
Version 12.2.0.1.1
OGGCORE_12.2.0.1.0_PLATFORMS_151211.1401_FBO
Linux, x64, 64bit (optimized), Oracle 12c on Dec 12 2015
02:56:48
Operating system character set identified as UTF-8.

Copyright (C) 1995, 2015, Oracle and/or its affiliates.
All rights reserved.

GGSCI (bigdata.localdomain) 1> DBLOGIN USERID ggate
Password:
Successfully logged into database.
GGSCI (bigdata.localdomain as ggate@bigdata) 2>
```

Next issue commands against schemas in the source database, configuring data capture on the source:

```
ADD SCHEMATRANDATA email
```

The result should look something like this:

```
GGSCI (bigdata.localdomain as ggate@bigdata) 2> ADD
```

```
SCHEMATRANDATA email
2016-11-11 01:00:57  INFO    OGG-01788  SCHEMATRANDATA has
been added on schema email.
2016-11-11 01:00:57  INFO    OGG-01976  SCHEMATRANDATA for
scheduling columns has been added on schema email.
GGSCI (bigdata.localdomain as ggate@bigdata) 3>
```

There are other options for schema-level supplemental logging:

```
ADD SCHEMATRANDATA <schema> [ ALLCOLS | NOSCHEDULINGCOLS ]
```

No options are used for the EMAIL schema above, which will force all primary keys to be logged even if unchanged (helps to locate unique rows), in addition to only logging foreign and unique key values if at least a foreign or unique key was changed in a database operation. The ALLCOLS option logs everything in all tables for a schema (all columns), every time something is changed in a row, which can create a lot of overhead by logging everything that is changed as well as everything that is not changed. The following command adds to a schema called BIGDATA:

```
ADD SCHEMATRANDATA bigdata ALLCOLS
```

and the result is as follows:

```
GGSCI (bigdata.localdomain as ggate@bigdata) 3> ADD
SCHEMATRANDATA bigdata ALLCOLS
2016-11-11 01:11:31  INFO    OGG-01788  SCHEMATRANDATA has
been added on schema bigdata.
2016-11-11 01:11:31  INFO    OGG-01976  SCHEMATRANDATA for
scheduling columns has been added on schema bigdata.
2016-11-11 01:11:31  INFO    OGG-01977  SCHEMATRANDATA for
all columns has been added on schema bigdata.
GGSCI (bigdata.localdomain as ggate@bigdata) 4>
```

Similarly, the NOSCHEDULINGCOLS option is the minimum for schema-level logging, logging only primary and unique index values (for valid indexes only). This is perhaps a more sensible option for a BigData environment because there is so much information being generated, but do not execute this line now (it is commented out for that reason):

```
--ADD SCHEMATRANDATA bigdata NOSCHEDULINGCOLS
```

Table-Level Supplemental Logging

First, table-level logging cannot be used within a schema that is schema-logging enabled; this is because schema-level logging overrides individual table-level logging. Second, table-level logging has the same default as schema-level logging when not using any options for the ADD SCHEMATRANDATA command. Thus primary keys are logged even if unchanged. Foreign and unique key values are only logged if at least a foreign or unique key was changed in a database operation:

```
ADD TRANDATA <schema>.<table>
```

Table-level supplemental logging uses the ADD TRANDATA command with the following options:

```
ADD TRANDATA <schema>.<table> [,COLS (columns)] [,NOKEY]
[,ALLCOLS|NOSCHEDULINGCOLS]
```

As with schema-level logging, the ALLCOLS option logs everything in a table every time something is changed in a row, and the NOSCHEDULINGCOLS option logs only primary and unique index values (for valid indexes only). The COLS option will log non-key columns that can be used for filtering and changes, as well as the primary key—unique indexes must be created on the target database for columns defined by the COLS clause. The NOKEY clause is added, which blocks primary and unique key logging (KEYCOLS clause required in a table). So one can add table-level logging to a single table as follows:

```
ADD TRANDATA dmevents.earthquake
```

And this is the response from GGSCI:

```
GGSCI (bigdata.localdomain as ggate@bigdata) 3> ADD
TRANDATA dmevents.earthquake

2016-11-14 00:51:55  WARNING OGG-06439  No unique key is
defined for table EARTHQUAKE. All viable columns will
```

be used to represent the key, but may not guarantee uniqueness. KEYCOLS may be used to define the key.

```
Logging of supplemental redo data enabled for table
DMEVENTS.EARTHQUAKE.
TRANDATA for scheduling columns has been added on table
'DMEVENTS.EARTHQUAKE'.
TRANDATA for instantiation CSN has been added on table
'DMEVENTS.EARTHQUAKE'.
GGSCI (bigdata.localdomain as ggate@bigdata) 4>
```

There is schema-level logging on EMAIL and BIDDATA schemas, as well as table-level logging on DMEVENTS schema tables. And this is the response from GGSCI for a table that does have uniqueness defined:

```
GGSCI (bigdata.localdomain as ggate@bigdata) 10> ADD
TRANDATA dmevents.volcano
```

```
Logging of supplemental redo data enabled for table
DMEVENTS.VOLCANO.
TRANDATA for scheduling columns has been added on table
'DMEVENTS.VOLCANO'.
TRANDATA for instantiation CSN has been added on table
'DMEVENTS.VOLCANO'.
GGSCI (bigdata.localdomain as ggate@bigdata) 11>
```

And this is the response from GGSCI for the table that already has a primary key, but the uniqueness combines the existing primary key and columns added by the column clause. In this case the intention is to augment the primary key, such as when a primary key is a surrogate; a surrogate key is often an integer auto-counter and to the naked eye is semantically meaningless:

```
GGSCI (bigdata.localdomain as ggate@bigdata) 25> ADD
TRANDATA dmevents.volcano COLS(name,magnitude)
```

```
2016-11-14 01:11:50  WARNING OGG-00706  Failed to add
```

```
supplemental log group on table DMEVENTS.VOLCANO due
to ORA-00957: duplicate column name SQL ALTER TABLE
"DMEVENTS"."VOLCANO" ADD SUPPLEMENTAL LOG GROUP "GGS_92635"
("NAME","ERUPTION","NAME","MAGNITUDE") ALWAYS  /*
GOLDENGATE_DDL_REPLICATION */.

TRANDATA for instantiation CSN has been added on table
'DMEVENTS.VOLCANO'.
GGSCI (bigdata.localdomain as ggate@bigdata) 26>
```

One can also not add too many columns with the COLS clause to enhance the uniqueness within a table, first deleting the previous definition to allow for replacement:

```
GGSCI (bigdata.localdomain as ggate@bigdata) 12> DELETE
TRANDATA dmevents.volcano

Logging of supplemental redo log data disabled for table
DMEVENTS.VOLCANO.
TRANDATA for scheduling columns has been disabled on table
'DMEVENTS.VOLCANO'.
GGSCI (bigdata.localdomain as ggate@bigdata) 13> ADD
TRANDATA dmevents.volcano COLS(magnitude)

Logging of supplemental redo data enabled for table
DMEVENTS.VOLCANO.
TRANDATA for scheduling columns has been added on table
'DMEVENTS.VOLCANO'.
TRANDATA for instantiation CSN has been added on table
'DMEVENTS.VOLCANO'.
GGSCI (bigdata.localdomain as ggate@bigdata) 27>
```

When implementing table-level logging, one can grant flashback to specific tables on a table-by-table basis from SQLPLUS:

```
sqlplus / as sysdba
GRANT FLASHBACK ON dmevents.volcano TO ggate;
```

2.4 So What's Next?

This chapter has demonstrated how to download and install GoldenGate software, as well as some basic Oracle Database configuration that is required to enable GoldenGate software. This information is important as a step in the process of showing how to build a basic GoldenGate installation. The next chapter digs into the configuration of capture and apply processing, where data change is captured on a source database and then applied on a target database.

Chapter 3

Configuring GoldenGate

The goal of this chapter is to go through the process of basic configuration of GoldenGate, including Capture and Apply, plus different types and combinations of Capture and Apply, leading into process groups and finally a brief test of replication in action.

3.1 The Architecture of Capture (Extract) and Apply (Replicat)

The capture process is the process that gathers information about changes to the source database—it extracts information as a record of changes made to the source database using the Extract process on the source database. The apply process applies changes onto the target database as they are extracted from the source—it replicates or duplicates changes to mimic changes made to the source onto the target database using the Replicat process.

GoldenGate calls the Extract process and its associated files a group, which can, but does not have to, include data pump processing, where data pump can be used to read source Extract trail files and send changes over a network to a target. Figure 3.1 shows a basic process flow from source to target of: (1) source capture (Extract) to local trail, (2) to data pump, (3) data pump across a network to a target remote trail, and (4) to apply (Replicat) on a target.

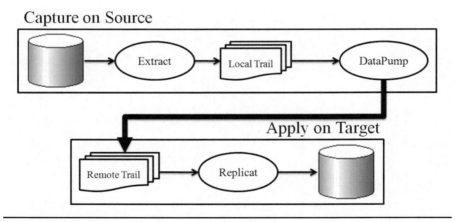

Figure 3.1 Basic GoldenGate Process Flow from Source to Target

3.1.1 Capture Method Architecture

There are two capture modes that Extract can execute with: (1) classic capture, and (2) integrated capture modes—the choice of which depends on specific issues between source and target databases, which includes data types, configuration of databases, and Oracle® Database versions.

Classic Capture

As shown in Figure 3.2, the GoldenGate capture Extract process reads Oracle Database archive and redo logs in order to generate changes from the source to pass to the target. Changes can optionally be pushed through a local trail and data pump process to help isolate source from target and reduce dependency in case of failure.

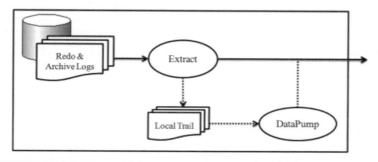

Figure 3.2   How Classic Capture Works on the Source

Classic capture does not support multitenant databases and has some restrictions with respect to complex data types, as described by the following URL in Chapter 1 of the Oracle GoldenGate Installation Guide for Oracle Database 12:

```
https://docs.oracle.com/goldengate/1212/gg-winux/GIORA/system_
requirements.htm#GIORA122
```

Integrated Capture

As shown in Figure 3.3, integrated capture is a more capable Extract method, with none of the restrictions of classic capture. Integrated capture works with Oracle Database Logminer processing, which reads the Oracle Database archive and redo log files, as opposed to reading only the logs directly. Thus the Logminer process interprets all the information properly to allow for more comprehensive and fully integrated data capture on the source.

> *Integrated Capture and Apply are intended for use with Oracle12c; non-integrated replication is used in Oracle11g and other databases.*

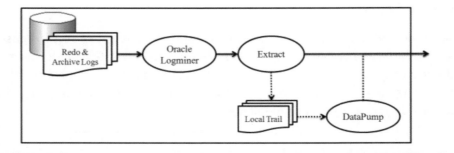

Figure 3.3   How Integrated Capture Works on the Source

3.1.2 Apply Method Architecture

As well as two capture modes, there are also two apply modes: (1) non-integrated, and (2) integrated; both modes use SQL coding and built-in Oracle Database Replication, and the latter includes Oracle Streams.

Non-Integrated Apply

As shown in Figure 3.4, non-integrated apply mode simply reads the trail of changes from the remote trail on the target server, and then applies those changes as SQL code DDL and DML statements executed against the target database. Non-integrated apply mode can execute multiple Replicat processes to move data in parallel. Non-integrated apply processing is generally more beneficial in small transactional change databases, such as online transaction processing (OLTP) type applications.

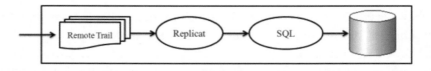

Figure 3.4   How Non-Integrated Apply Works on the s

Integrated Replicat Apply

As shown in Figure 3.5, integrated apply mode uses Oracle Replication and Streams technology to allow creation of coordinated Apply processes that move changes to a target database in parallel, asynchronously and automatically coordinating between multiple apply processes without conflict in the sequence of transactions. The resulting effect is that integrated apply mode is best for parallel operations that involve large amounts of I/O loads. The perfect example of this type of database is a data warehouse database, in that data warehouses are often heavily partitioned databases with large I/O transactions that easily benefit from automated asynchronous splitting of change across multiple apply process threads; in other words, parallel processing partitioned databases with heavy I/O load.

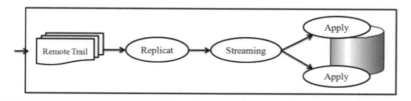

Figure 3.5   How Integrated Apply Works on the Target

3.1.3 Mixing Methods of Capture and Apply

A discussion of mixing the various capture and apply methods is out of the scope of this book, but it is important to note that classic capture does not have to include an Oracle database at the source—it does at the target. The reasons for this are that integrated capture is custom built for Oracle Database and caters to all of Oracle's complex and unusual data types; those extra data types are often not present or perhaps are built differently in other relational databases.

> *The Oracle12c recommended configuration for Golden Gate is integrated capture on an Oracle source database, replicating to integrated Replicat on an Oracle target database. Also, the target database executes a single Replicat process for each source database involved.*

3.2 Configuring Classic Capture

Configuration of classic capture involves a parameter file that is applied to the process, which implements the capturing function—it is called the

Extract process. The parameter file must be created on the source database server by connecting to GGSCI, and then creating the Extract process parameter file as shown below:

```
cd $ORACLE_GG
ggsci
edit params ext1
```

And now create the Extract process parameter file for a schema called BIGDATA in the source database, including the LOGALLSUPCOLS parameter to ensure that logs are captured with all detail on the source server:

```
--define the extract process
EXTRACT ext1
--connect as a DDL supporting database user
USERID ggate, PASSWORD ggate
--this is the extract trail on the source
EXTTRAIL /u01/app/oracle/product/12.1.0/oggcore_1/dirdat/lt
--this is for DML capturing all tables and all sequences in
  the bigdata schema
TABLE bigdata.*;
SEQUENCE bigdata.*;
--setting up DDL support for all objects in the bigdata user
LOGALLSUPCOLS
DDL INCLUDE MAPPED OBJNAME bigdata.*
```

DDL capture is enabled using the DDL parameter, where DDL is explicitly included or excluded, as in this example from above:

```
DDL INCLUDE MAPPED OBJNAME bigdata.*
```

Including the DDL parameter in the Extract parameter file captures and applies all DDL commands, depending on specifically detailed DDL requirements for GoldenGate replication, the specifics of which are well beyond the scope of this book and can be found at this link:

```
https://docs.oracle.com/goldengate/1212/gg-winux/GIORA/ddl.
htm#GIORA959
```

> *DDL support is cited on many websites requiring various procedures be executed, which applies to pre-Oracle12c Database versions only.*

3.2.1 Adding Data Pump to the Extract Configuration

Figure 3.1 showed that data pump optionally connects the local trail on the source server to the remote trail on a target server. Data pump is optional, but it creates a logging trail, and thus the same parameter file contains connection information to a target server. Editing these parameters:

```
edit params ext1
```

and change by adding data pump configuration to the existing extract configuration:

```
--hostname and port for trail )(define in /etc/hosts). 7809 is
   default port for GoldenGate
RMTHOST failover, MGRPORT 7809
--path and name for trail (as per create subdirs on target as
   in Chapter 2)
RMTTRAIL /u01/app/oracle/product/12.1.0/oggcore_1/dirdat/rt
```

Now check the manager process parameters:

```
edit params mgr
```

This should be in the file as defined above for the RMTHOST setting:

```
PORT 7809
```

Next add configuration parameters for Extract, data pump, the manager process, and the remote trail on a target server. Examining the parameter files subdirectory (subdir) on the source server should show all the files and their contents:

```
[oracle@bigdata.localdomain dirdat-bigdata]$ cd /u01/app/
oracle/product/12.1.0/oggcore_1/dirprm
```

```
[oracle@bigdata.localdomain dirprm-bigdata]$ ls -la
total 16
drwxr-x---  2 oracle oinstall 4096 Dec 24 16:47 .
drwxr-xr-x 26 oracle oinstall 4096 Jul 27 11:20 ..
-rw-r-----  1 oracle oinstall  702 Dec 24 16:47 ext1.prm
-rw-r--r--  1 oracle oinstall    9 Jul 27 11:20 mgr.prm
[oracle@bigdata.localdomain dirprm-bigdata]$ cat mgr.prm
PORT 7809
[oracle@bigdata.localdomain dirprm-bigdata]$ cat ext1.prm
--define the extract process
EXTRACT ext1
--connect as a DDL supporting database user
USERID ggate, PASSWORD ggate
--this is the extract trail on the source
EXTTRAIL /u01/app/oracle/product/12.1.0/oggcore_1/dirdat/lt
--this is for DML capturing all tables and all sequences in
  the bigdata schema
LOGALLSUPCOLS
TABLE bigdata.*;
SEQUENCE bigdata.*;
--setting up DDL support for all objects in the bigdata schema
DDL INCLUDE MAPPED OBJNAME bigdata.*

--hostname and port for trail )(define in /etc/hosts). 7809 is
  default port for GoldenGate
RMTHOST failover, mgrport 7809
--path and name for trail (as per create subdirs on target as
  in Chapter 2
RMTTRAIL /u01/app/oracle/product/12.1.0/oggcore_1/dirdat/lt
```

Connect to GGSCI again, and see what is running by executing a simple command to display all currently available information:

```
cd $ORACLE_GG
ggsci
info all
```

Something like the following should result:

```
GGSCI (bigdata.localdomain) 1> info all
```

```
Program     Status      Group     Lag at Chkpt   Time Since Chkpt
MANAGER     STOPPED
GGSCI (bigdata.localdomain) 2>
```

3.2.2 Limitations of Classic Capture

Classic capture is limited in a number ways, including Transparent Data Encryption (TDE), Oracle RAC, Automatic Storage Management (ASM), data availability, archived log mode, Oracle Data Guard, and log bottlenecks. Classic capture requires more manual involvement and complexity than integrated capture:

- **Transparent Data Encryption (TDE).** Classic capture uses Oracle logmining to enable TDE between source and target, and requires encryption key exchanges between source and target, as well as some extra procedure executions.
- **Oracle Real Application Clusters (RAC).** Classic capture leaves out some complexities otherwise resolved by integrated capture.
- **Automated Storage Management (ASM).** There are some classic capture complexities reading logs, as well as some complexities with Oracle Data Vault. The TRANSLOGOPTIONS parameter set to the DBLOGREADER option is used in the Extract process parameter file.
- **Availability of Data.** This implies that data must always be available on the source for the Extract process to capture. Use archive log mode to prevent rapidly recycling redo logs causing entries to be missed by the Extract process. An Oracle Database that is not in archived log mode is at risk and not recommended. RMAN can be used to retain older logs, but archivelog mode is still a requirement.
- **Archive Log Only Mode.** Classic capture can be configured to read from archive logs only, excluding redo logs. This method is not configurable in integrated capture mode, and there are some limitations using Archive Log Only (ALO) mode only when Oracle RAC is involved.
- **Active Data Guard (ADG) Only Mode.** Classic capture mode can Extract metadata as well as log data in real-time using Oracle ADG.
- **Log Read Bottlenecks.** These can occur because a source database is writing to redo logs at the same time that the Extract process is reading from those same redo log files; this creates significant I/O bottleneck problems. The only solution is faster hardware for redo logs (faster disks and faster disk controllers), or perhaps something like RAID that does not include parity.

3.3 Configuring Integrated Capture

Configuration of integrated capture involves a parameter file applied to the process, which implements the capturing function called the Extract process. An important difference to understand is that the mining process does not have to be instantiated on the source server and can be implemented further down the replication event chain.

A multitenant database is simply treated as being multiple source and target databases, except that GoldenGate parameter files reference generic objects using the container databases.

The Extract process parameter file can be created on the source database server as follows, beginning by connecting to GGSCI to create the Extract process parameter file:

```
cd $ORACLE_GG
ggsci
edit params ext1
```

As with the classic capture configuration, the Extract process parameters are the same, with the only change being the DDL INCLUDE MAPPED setting that simply includes everything:

```
--define the extract process
EXTRACT ext1
--connect as a DDL supporting database user
USERID ggate, PASSWORD ggate
--this is the extract trail on the source
EXTTRAIL /u01/app/oracle/product/12.1.0/oggcore_1/dirdat/lt
--this is for DML capturing all tables and all sequences in
  the bigdata schema
LOGALLSUPCOLS
TABLE bigdata.*;
SEQUENCE bigdata.*;
--setting up DDL support for all objects
DDL INCLUDE MAPPED
```

Changes for a multitenant database require that objects are accessible by container database using the addition of the SOURCECATALOG parameter—for example, one could configure something such as this:

```
--for a pluggable database called CONTAINER1
SOURCECATALOG CONTAINER1
TABLE dmevents.*;
TABLE dmfinance.*;
--for a pluggable database called CONTAINER2
SOURCECATALOG CONTAINER2
TABLE bigdata.*;
TABLE email.*;
DDL INCLUDE MAPPED SOURCECATALOG CONTAINER1 INCLUDE MAPPED
SOURCECATALOG CONTAINER2
```

The logmining function can be placed on the source database or further down the replication chain, which requires specialized changes to Extract parameters using the TRANSLOGOPTIONS parameter.

Configuring the logmining function to mine log files away from the source database can be useful to separate functionality and create a more robust architecture, such as mining (reading) log files from a standby server. The result is the removal of the logmining processing from a busy source system, which is beyond the scope of this book.

Adding data pump to the Extract process configuration is the same for both classic and integrated capture.

3.4 Configuring Apply

The Replicat process is the application of change on the target side of the replication process within GoldenGate, executing transactions on a target database as captured on and copied from a source database. Much like the Extract process, the Replicat process is configured using a parameter file on the target server that determines the behavior of the Replicat process.

The first step is to execute GGSCI on the target server and create a Replicat process parameter file as in the following:

```
cd $ORACLE_GG
ggsci
edit params rep1
```

Next add the appropriate parameters inside GGSCI where the ASSUMETARGETDEFS parameter applies the assumption that tables on source and target have the same metadata definitions and structure—the SOURCEDEFS parameter allows for mapping of differences:

```
--define the replicat process
REPLICAT rep1
--connect as a DDL supporting database user
USERID ggate, PASSWORD ggate
ASSUMETARGETDEFS
--source and target databases use the same schema names in
  this case
MAP bigdata.*, TARGET bigdata.*;
```

The MAP parameter maps from source to target database objects using the following structure:

```
MAP [container.]<schema.><object>, TARGET <schema.>object;
```

Also, the optional DBOPTIONS INTEGRATEDPARAMS parameter settings allow for specialized integrated parameter settings. Non-integrated and integrated modes are the same with this configuration; the parameter can be added as follows:

```
--define the replicat process
REPLICAT rep1
--connect as a DDL supporting database user
USERID ggate, PASSWORD ggate
ASSUMETARGETDEFS
DBOPTIONS INTEGRATEDPARAMS(PARALLELISM 2)
--source and target databases use the same schema names in
  this case
```

```
MAP bigdata.*, TARGET bigdata.*;
```

> *Given the limited scope of this book, assume integrated Extract and integrated Replicat have the most sensible configuration options for simplicity in the use of the latest version of Oracle (12c), on both source and target servers.*

3.4.1 Limitations of Non-Integrated Apply

There are some limitations that are appropriate to the choice of configuring with non-integrated Apply, and they are as follows:

- **Checkpoint Table.** Required for non-integrated Replicat but not for integrated Replicat. The checkpoint table is configured on the target database as follows, first by editing a GLOBAL parameter file:

```
cd $ORACLE_GG
ggsci
edit params ./GLOBAL
```

and adding the following and saving:

```
GGSCHEMA ggate
CHECKPOINTTABLE ggate.CHECKPOINT
```

then connecting as the same user and adding the checkpoint table:

```
DBLOGIN USERID ggate, PASSWORD ggate
ADD CHECKPOINTTABLE ggate.CHECKPOINT
```

shown by the following executed commands:

```
GGSCI (failover.localdomain) 2> DBLOGIN USERID ggate, PASSWORD
ggate
Successfully logged into database.

GGSCI (failover.localdomain as ggate@failover) 3> ADD
CHECKPOINTTABLE ggate.CHECKPOINT
```

```
Successfully created checkpoint table ggate.CHECKPOINT.

GGSCI (failover.localdomain as ggate@failover) 4>
```

The checkpoint table and GLOBAL file can be re-moved to implement Integrated Capture for Oracle12c Database.

```
GGSCI (failover.localdomain as ggate@failover) 5> delete
checkpointtable ggate.CHECKPOINT
This checkpoint table may be required for other installations.
Are you sure you want to delete this checkpoint table? yes

Successfully deleted checkpoint table ggate.CHECKPOINT.
```

Remove the checkpoint table from the parameter file as follows:

```
GGSCI (failover.localdomain as ggate@failover) 7> edit params
./GLOBAL
```

- **Disable Triggers and Referential Integrity on Target Tables.** In non-integrated Apply mode, triggers and cascading constraints must be disabled in the target database. Triggers and cascading constraints are very out of date and not generally compatible with large-scale or complex modern databases.
- **Constraint Checking on Target Tables.** This option is even more risky than the option above (Disable Triggers and Referential Integrity on Target Tables), because constraints may have to be deferred, which implies a potential for replication of inconsistent data.

3.5 Configuration Limitations for Both Capture and Apply

There are some specific configuration issues related to row uniqueness, Oracle Database sequences, complex data types, as well as some specific objects and commands—all are detailed as follows:

- **Unique Rows.** In order for a row to be locatable by a change replicated from the source, a source and target table undergoing an UPDATE or DELETE statement must have a unique value to use that exists on both source and target. Without a unique value, a row cannot be located. In order of decreasing precedence, unless indicated otherwise, GoldenGate will use the primary key followed by the first unique key (with data type restrictions). If no key exists, GoldenGate creates a unique key of all usable columns, excluding some specialized data types that can create a large amount of overhead. In short, create primary keys on tables or your system may suffer some serious performance issues. As another option, the Extract TABLE and Replicat MAP parameters allow the inclusion of a KEYCOLS clause, which permits a table to have a specific set of columns defined for uniqueness if primary and unique keys are unwanted or not present.
- **Oracle Database Sequences.** Oracle sequences are auto counters that require specific configuration in GoldenGate on both the source and target databases:

```
cd $ORACLE_GG
ggsci
edit params ./GLOBAL
GGSCHEMA ggate
```

Still in the $ORACLE_GG home directory, execute the sequence.sql script in SQLPLUS on the source, entering the GGATE user when prompted:

```
SQLPLUS / AS SYSDBA
@sequence.sql
```

It looks like this:

```
SQL> @sequence.sql
Please enter the name of a schema for the GoldenGate database
objects:
ggate
Setting schema name to GGATE
```

Execute the following grant on the source database in SQLPLUS:

```
GRANT EXECUTE on ggate .updateSequence to
bigdata,email,dmevents;
```

and on the target by selecting the GGATE user for the target:

```
SQLPLUS / AS SYSDBA
@sequence.sql
GRANT EXECUTE on ggate .updateSequence to
bigdata,email,dmevents;
```

Lastly, on the source database in SQLPLUS, you have to make the following change to ensure that sequence changes are forcibly logged in the source server but are also able to automatically replicate to the target as they change on the source:

```
ALTER TABLE sys.seq$ ADD SUPPLEMENTAL LOG DATA (PRIMARY KEY)
COLUMNS;
```

- **Issues with Complex Data Types.** There are specific issues with respect to replicating complex data types, including multi byte strings, spatial objects, timestamps, LOBs, XML types, and user-defined types. Potential solutions can be found at this URL:

```
https://docs.oracle.com/goldengate/1212/gg-winux/GIORA/
additional_config.htm#GIORA376
```

- **Issues with Objects.** There are specific issues when replicating certain types of infrequently used objects, as well as certain types of operations on those objects. Included are interval partitioned tables, virtual columns, updatable views, mapping redo and archive logs to separate locations on source and target (never a sensible option), TRUNCATE command issues, and DDL on sequences, there is more information at this URL:

```
https://docs.oracle.com/goldengate/1212/gg-winux/GIORA/
additional_config.htm#GIORA383
```

3.6 Process Group Configuration

Configuration of process groups involves adding all the pieces that make up the replication process. The pieces include a minimum of a single primary Extract process group, a single data pump process group, and a single Replicat process group. This discussion will cover a little more than just those three, including how to register the Extract process group with data mining on the source, adding the primary Extract on the source, adding the local trail on the source, adding the data pump Extract group on the source, adding the remote trail on a target, and finally adding the Replicat group on a target.

- **Register Extract with Data Mining on the Source.** Integrated Apply needs registration of the Extract process with the logmining server on the source database:

```
DBLOGIN USERID ggate
REGISTER EXTRACT ext1 DATABASE
```

and the result would look something like this:

```
GGSCI (bigdata.localdomain) 3> DBLOGIN USERID ggate
Password:
Successfully logged into database.
GGSCI (bigdata.localdomain as ggate@bigdata) 4> REGISTER
EXTRACT ext1 DATABASE
2017-01-13 02:04:29  INFO    OGG-02003  Extract EXT1
successfully registered with database at SCN 3998529.
```

If there are errors with existing extracts and the Extract process has been registered more than once, it might become necessary to find the offending process and kill it. There are also CONTAINER and SCN options for multiple pluggable container databases, where one can begin the Extract process at a particular SCN; omitting the SCN option starts the Extract at the point that the Extract process is registered.

```
REGISTER EXTRACT <name> DATABASE [ CONTAINER(db1, db2) ] [SCN
<scn> ]
```

- **Add Primary Extract on the Source.** Capture data as it occurs on the source by adding the Extract process as follows:

```
ADD EXTRACT ext1 INTEGRATED TRANLOG BEGIN NOW
```

Other options are as follows:

```
ADD EXTRACT <name>
{ TRANLOG | INTEGRATED TRANLOG }
{ BEGIN { NOW | yyyy-mm-dd[ hh:mi:ss ] | SCN }
[ THREADS n ]
```

TRANLOG applies classic capture. BEGIN implies extract processing starts at a specific time stamp or SCN, or at the point of Extract process addition. The THREADS option is used for multiple redo log threads and classic capture mode in Oracle RAC.

- **Adding Local Trail on Source.** The automatically created local trail has source captured data written to it by the Extract process:

```
ADD EXTTRAIL /u01/app/oracle/product/12.1.0/oggcore_1/dirdat/
lt, EXTRACT ext1
```

- **Adding Remote Trail on Source.** The remote trail is placed on the source server and uses data pump to talk to the target:

```
ADD RMTTRAIL /u01/app/oracle/product/12.1.0/oggcore_1/dirdat/
rt, EXTRACT ext1
```

- **Adding Replicat on Target.** The Replicat process runs on the target, reading changes from the remote trail and re-executing (replicating) those changes on the target system:

```
DBLOGIN USERID ggate
ADD REPLICAT rep1 INTEGRATED, EXTTRAIL /u01/app/oracle/
product/12.1.0/oggcore_1/dirdat/rt
```

There are three points to note: (1) the INTEGRATED option can be omitted to use classic Capture, (2) the external trail (EXTTRAIL) is the remote trail on the source machine, and (3) the Replicat process (REPLICAT parameter) is allowed a maximum 8 character length name. The result would look something like this:

```
GGSCI (failover.localdomain as ggate@failover) 3> ADD REPLICAT
rep1 INTEGRATED, EXTTRAIL /u01/app/oracle/product/12.1.0/
oggcore_1/dirdat/rt
REPLICAT (Integrated) added.


GGSCI (failover.localdomain as ggate@failover) 4> info all

Program     Status       Group      Lag at Chkpt   Time Since Chkpt


MANAGER     STOPPED
REPLICAT    STOPPED      REPL1      00:00:00       00:00:07
GGSCI (failover.localdomain as ggate@failover) 5>
```

3.7 Starting Up Oracle GoldenGate Replication

The current configuration so far in this book is for the source server with the Extract parameter file as follows:

```
EXTRACT ext1
USERID ggate, PASSWORD ggate
EXTTRAIL /u01/app/oracle/product/12.1.0/oggcore_1/dirdat/lt
TABLE bigdata.*;
SEQUENCE bigdata.*;
DDL INCLUDE MAPPED
LOGALLSUPCOLS
RMTHOST failover, mgrport 7809
RMTTRAIL /u01/app/oracle/product/12.1.0/oggcore_1/dirdat/rt
```

and the Replicat parameters placed on the target server as follows:

```
REPLICAT rep1
USERID ggate, PASSWORD ggate
ASSUMETARGETDEFS
DBOPTIONS INTEGRATEDPARAMS(PARALLELISM 2)
MAP bigdata.*, TARGET bigdata.*;
```

Initially a typing (spelling) error was placed in the Replicat parameter file where the PARALLELISM parameter was typed incorrectly as PARRELIM and the GGSCI utility log file was scanned to isolate the error using this command:

```
VIEW GGSEVT
```

Scrolling to the bottom of the log file the exact error was located, shown in the sequence below that leads to the exact description of the error:

```
2017-01-16 15:51:45  INFO    OGG-00995  Oracle GoldenGate
Delivery for Oracle, rep1.prm:  REPLICAT REP1 starting.
2017-01-16 15:51:45  INFO    OGG-03059  Oracle GoldenGate
Delivery for Oracle, rep1.prm:  Operating system character set
identified as UTF-8.
2017-01-16 15:51:45  INFO    OGG-02695  Oracle GoldenGate
Delivery for Oracle, rep1.prm:  ANSI SQL parameter syntax is
used for parameter parsing.
2017-01-16 15:51:45  ERROR   OGG-10141  Oracle GoldenGate
Delivery for Oracle, rep1.prm:  (rep1.prm) line 6 column 28:
Parsing error, value "'PARALLELIM'" syntax error.
2017-01-16 15:51:45  ERROR   OGG-01668  Oracle GoldenGate
Delivery for Oracle, rep1.prm:  PROCESS
ABENDING.
```

Viewing errors is important, and the VIEW GGSEVT command is a useful option to start with in finding simplistic errors. As a result of consistent errors with the configuration built so far in this book, it makes sense to revert to a simpler configuration using integrated Extract on the source and non-integrated Replicat on the target. There is some possibility indicated by Google searching that integrated Replicat has bugs in Oracle Database and Oracle GoldenGate 12.1.0.2. The easy way to solve this problem is to get around it by rebuilding from scratch—see Chapter 7 for deinstalling and reinstalling GoldenGate from scratch. Note that Chapter 2 shows how to add the various layers of supplemental logging for the BIGDATA, EMAIL, and DMEVENTS schemas that are removed by dropping and recreating the GGATE tablespace and the GGATE user.

3.7.1 *Deinstall and Rebuild Replication*

Stop all GGSCI processes on source and target:

```
ggsci
stop ER *
stop manager
```

Remove the Extract and Replicat processes on source and target. On the source:

```
UNREGISTER EXTRACT ext1 DATABASE
DELETE EXTRACT ext1
```

and on the target:

```
UNREGISTER REPLICAT rep1 DATABASE
DELETE REPLICAT rep1
```

Remove all the schema and table-level supplemental logging, because it is stored with the GGATE username inside the source database and the GGATE user will be recreated:

```
ggsci
DBLOGIN USERID ggate, password ggate
DELETE TRANDATA dmevents.earthquake
DELETE TRANDATA dmevents.volcano
DELETE SCHEMATRANDATA email
DELETE SCHEMATRANDATA bigdata
```

Now remove DDL replication procedures on the source:

```
sqlplus / as sysdba
@ddl_disable.sql;
@ddl_remove.sql;
@marker_remove.sql;
```

Remove GoldenGate software on both servers:

```
/u01/app/oracle/product/12.1.0/oggcore_1/deinstall/deinstall.sh
```

and now drop and recreate the GGATE tablespace and user from the source (it might be necessary to restart a database to forcibly disconnect processes):

```
DROP USER ggate CASCADE;
DROP TABLESPACE ggate INCLUDING CONTENTS AND DATAFILES;
CREATE BIGFILE TABLESPACE ggate
DATAFILE '/u02/app/oracle/oradata/bigdata/ggate01.dbf' SIZE 1G
AUTOEXTEND ON;
CREATE USER ggate IDENTIFIED BY ggate
DEFAULT TABLESPACE ggate TEMPORARY TABLESPACE TEMP;
GRANT DBA, CONNECT, RESOURCE, UNLIMITED TABLESPACE TO ggate;
GRANT EXECUTE ON UTL_FILE TO ggate;
GRANT FLASHBACK ANY TABLE TO ggate;
```

and on the target:

```
DROP USER ggate CASCADE;
DROP TABLESPACE ggate INCLUDING CONTENTS AND DATAFILES;
CREATE BIGFILE TABLESPACE ggate
DATAFILE '/u02/app/oracle/oradata/failover/ggate01.dbf' SIZE
1G AUTOEXTEND ON;
CREATE USER ggate IDENTIFIED BY ggate
DEFAULT TABLESPACE ggate TEMPORARY TABLESPACE TEMP;
GRANT DBA, CONNECT, RESOURCE, UNLIMITED TABLESPACE TO ggate;
GRANT EXECUTE ON UTL_FILE TO ggate;
GRANT FLASHBACK ANY TABLE TO ggate;
```

Next reinstall GoldenGate as described in Chapter 7, and set up the schema- and table-level logging as added at the end of Chapter 7:

```
cd $ORACLE_GG
ggsci
DBLOGIN USERID ggate, PASSWORD ggate
ADD SCHEMATRANDATA email
ADD SCHEMATRANDATA bigdata ALLCOLS
ADD TRANDATA dmevents.earthquake
```

```
ADD TRANDATA dmevents.volcano COLS(magnitude)
```

3.7.2 A Simple Installation of Extract and Replicat

Let's begin by running the GoldenGate scripts that support DDL replication on the source database only:

```
cd $ORACLE_GG
sqlplus / as sysdba
SQL> @marker_setup.sql
SQL> @ddl_setup.sql
SQL> @role_setup.sql
SQL> grant GGS_GGSUSER_ROLE to ggate;
SQL> @ddl_enable.sql
```

> *The marker_setup.sql, ddl_setup.sql and role_setup.sql scripts all require an input of the central metadata schema, which in this case is the GGATE schema.*

Create an extraction user on the source:

```
create user capture identified by capture default tablespace
users temporary tablespace temp;
grant connect,resource,unlimited tablespace to capture;
```

and create an application user on the source:

```
create user appli identified by appli default tablespace users
temporary tablespace temp;
grant connect,resource,unlimited tablespace to appli;
```

> *appli is used because "apply" is a reserved word in Oracle Database.*

Start the manager on the source and target:

```
ggsci
info all
```

If the manager process is not listed as running then start the manager process:

```
START MANAGER
```

with the result as follows:

```
GGSCI (bigdata.localdomain) 2> info all
Program     Status     Group     Lag at Chkpt   Time Since Chkpt
MANAGER     RUNNING
```

Create the Extract process on the source and the extract trail on the source, and link it into the Extract process, and finally edit to create to the extract parameters on the source:

```
ADD EXTRACT ext1, TRANLOG, BEGIN NOW
ADD EXTTRAIL /u01/app/oracle/product/12.1.0/oggcore_1/dirdat/
lt, EXTRACT ext1
EDIT PARAMS ext1
```

and this is the content of the ext1 extract parameters file:

```
EXTRACT ext1
USERID ggate, password ggate
rmthost failover, mgrport 7809
rmttrail /u01/app/oracle/product/12.1.0/oggcore_1/dirdat/lt
--This supports collection of DDL from the CAPTURE schema
ddl include mapped objname capture.*
--This supports collection of DML from the CAPTURE schema
table capture.*;
```

Next move onto the target server to create the checkpoint table (non-integrated replication), by editing the ./GLOBAL parameters file, adding the checkpoint table in GGSCI, adding the Replicat process, and finally creating the Replicat process parameters:

```
ggsci
EDIT PARAMS ./GLOBAL
```

and add these lines to the ./GLOBAL parameters file:

```
GGSCHEMA ggate
CHECKPOINTTABLE ggate.CHECKPOINT
```

Now connect as the GGATE user in GGSCI:

```
DBLOGIN USERID ggate, PASSWORD ggate
ADD CHECKPOINTTABLE ggate.CHECKPOINT
```

Add the Replicat group and link between the extract trail and the check-point table:

```
ADD REPLICAT rep1, EXTTRAIL /u01/app/oracle/product/12.1.0/
oggcore_1/dirdat/lt, CHECKPOINTTABLE ggate.CHECKPOINT
```

and edit the Replicat parameters file:

```
EDIT PARAMS rep1
```

and this is the Replicat parameter file on the target:

```
REPLICAT rep1
ASSUMETARGETDEFS
USERID ggate, PASSWORD ggate
DISCARDFILE /u01/app/oracle/product/12.1.0/oggcore_1/dirdat/
rep1_discard.txt, APPEND, MEGABYTES 10
DDL
--Maps tables from source to target
MAP CAPTURE.*, TARGET APPLI.*;
```

Now start the Extract process on the source:

```
START EXTRACT ext1
```

Once again, using the INFO ALL command, the result should look like this:

```
GGSCI (bigdata.localdomain) 15> info all
Program       Status     Group       Lag at Chkpt   Time Since Chkpt
MANAGER       RUNNING
EXTRACT       RUNNING    EXT1        00:00:00       00:33:50
```

and start the Replicat process on the target:

```
START REPLICAT rep1
```

and, using the INFO ALL command, the result should look like this:

```
GGSCI (failover.localdomain as ggate@failover) 20> info all
Program       Status     Group       Lag at Chkpt   Time Since Chkpt
MANAGER       RUNNING
REPLICAT      RUNNING    REP1        00:00:00       00:00:00
```

Test the Replication Process

Test on the source in SQLPLUS:

```
sqlplus / as sysdba
CONNECT capture/capture@bigdata
CREATE TABLE test(id INTEGER PRIMARY KEY);
INSERT INTO test(id) VALUES(1);
COMMIT;
```

and on the target, but do not expect an instant replication, as it may take a few minutes to replicate change to the target:

```
sqlplus appli/appli@failover

SQL*Plus: Release 12.1.0.2.0 Production on Tue Mar 14 15:03:06 2017
Copyright (c) 1982, 2014, Oracle.  All rights reserved.
Last Successful login time: Tue Mar 14 2017 15:02:45 -04:00
Connected to:
Oracle Database 12c Enterprise Edition Release 12.1.0.2.0 -
64bit Production
With the Partitioning, OLAP, Advanced Analytics and Real
Application Testing options
```

```
SQL> select * from test;
        ID
----------
         1
```

As a final test, all the initial schemas described and logged in Chapter 7 can be added into the replication process, beginning with editing the Extract parameters file on the source:

```
EXTRACT ext1
USERID ggate, password ggate
rmthost failover, mgrport 7809
rmttrail /u01/app/oracle/product/12.1.0/oggcore_1/dirdat/lt
ddl include mapped objname capture.*, include mapped objname
bigdata.*, include mapped objname email.*, include mapped
objname dmevents.*
table capture.*;
table bigdata.*;
table email.*;
table dmevents.*;
```

and editing the Replicat parameters file on the target:

```
REPLICAT rep1
ASSUMETARGETDEFS
USERID ggate, PASSWORD ggate
DISCARDFILE /u01/app/oracle/product/12.1.0/oggcore_1/dirdat/
rep1_discard.txt, APPEND, MEGABYTES 10
DDL
--Maps tables from source to target
MAP CAPTURE.*, TARGET APPLI.*;
MAP bigdata.*, TARGET bigdata.*;
MAP email.*, TARGET email.*;
MAP dmevents.*, TARGET dmevents.*;
```

Start the manager processes on both the source and the target if they are currently stopped:

```
start mgr
```

Stop and start the Extract process on the source:

```
GGSCI (bigdata.localdomain) 15> stop extract ext1
Sending STOP request to EXTRACT EXT1 ...
Request processed.
GGSCI (bigdata.localdomain) 16> start extract ext1
Sending START request to MANAGER ...
EXTRACT EXT1 starting
GGSCI (bigdata.localdomain) 17> info all
Program      Status      Group      Lag at Chkpt   Time Since Chkpt
MANAGER      RUNNING
EXTRACT      RUNNING     EXT1       00:00:00       00:00:07
```

Stop and start the Replicat process on the target:

```
GGSCI (failover.localdomain) 6> stop replicat rep1
Request processed.
GGSCI (failover.localdomain) 7> start replicat rep1
Sending START request to MANAGER ...
REPLICAT REP1 starting
GGSCI (failover.localdomain) 8> info all
Program      Status      Group      Lag at Chkpt   Time Since Chkpt
MANAGER      RUNNING
REPLICAT     RUNNING     REP1       00:00:00       23:31:38
```

Grant all necessary privileges to each of the schemas on both source and target:

```
sqlplus / as sysdba

GRANT CONNECT, RESOURCE, UNLIMITED TABLESPACE TO bigdata;
GRANT CONNECT, RESOURCE, UNLIMITED TABLESPACE TO email;
GRANT CONNECT, RESOURCE, UNLIMITED TABLESPACE TO dmevents;
```

Run these on the source for all schemas in the source database:

```
sqlplus / nolog
CONNECT bigdata@bigdata
CREATE TABLE test(id INTEGER PRIMARY KEY);
```

```
INSERT INTO test(id) VALUES(1);
INSERT INTO test(id) VALUES(2);
INSERT INTO test(id) VALUES(3);
COMMIT;
CONNECT email@bigdata
CREATE TABLE test(id INTEGER PRIMARY KEY);
INSERT INTO test(id) VALUES(1);
INSERT INTO test(id) VALUES(2);
INSERT INTO test(id) VALUES(3);
COMMIT;
CONNECT dmevents@bigdata
CREATE TABLE test(id INTEGER PRIMARY KEY);
INSERT INTO test(id) VALUES(1);
INSERT INTO test(id) VALUES(2);
INSERT INTO test(id) VALUES(3);
COMMIT;
```

---

*If the TEST table is dropped on the source and does not
exist on the target, then the replication will stall as a result
of not being synchronized. One can simply create the
TEST table on the target to allow the replication process
to complete.*

Connecting to the target should show the data in the schema for the
TEST table:

```
[oracle@failover.localdomain oggcore_1-failover]$ sqlplus
bigdata@failover
SQL*Plus: Release 12.1.0.2.0 Production on Sat Mar 25 14:38:25
2017
Copyright (c) 1982, 2014, Oracle.  All rights reserved.
Enter password:
Last Successful login time: Fri Mar 24 2017 13:58:02 -04:00

Connected to:
Oracle Database 12c Enterprise Edition Release 12.1.0.2.0 -
64bit Production
```

```
With the Partitioning, OLAP, Advanced Analytics and Real
Application Testing options

SQL> select * from test;
        ID
----------
         1
         2
         3
SQL>
```

3.8 So What's Next?

This chapter has demonstrated how to configure the basics of GoldenGate, including both Capture and Apply sides of the replication process. This information is important because after installation in the previous chapter, this chapter extends into modifying that installation by configuring what has been installed so far. The next chapter changes from the architectural setup of the first three chapters onto administering GoldenGate as a currently running system.

Chapter 4

Basic GoldenGate Administration

The goal of this chapter is to describe the basics of GoldenGate administration, in addition to that already covered in previous chapters. This chapter is divided up between coverage of configuring GoldenGate credentials, using the GGSCI command line tool, and finally a brief section on backups.

4.1 Configuring Credentials for GoldenGate

Parameter files for Extract and Replicat processes can access source and target databases, as specified in their respective parameter files on each server as follows:

```
USERID ggate, PASSWORD ggate
```

One can also specify an Oracle® TNS name to connect to a database, allowing, for instance, to replicate between source and target databases on the same server. The following can be added to the Extract parameter file:

```
USERID ggate@bigdata, PASSWORD ggate
```

and the following into the Replicat parameter file:

```
USERID ggate@failover, PASSWORD ggate
```

where the tnsnames.ora configuration contains two TNS name configuration definitions like these:

```
BIGDATA =
  (DESCRIPTION =
    (ADDRESS = (PROTOCOL = TCP)(HOST = bigdata.localdomain)
    (PORT = 1742))
    (CONNECT_DATA = (SERVER = DEDICATED) (SERVICE_NAME =
     bigdata))
  )

FAILOVER =
  (DESCRIPTION =
    (ADDRESS = (PROTOCOL = TCP)(HOST = failover.localdomain)
    (PORT = 1863))
    (CONNECT_DATA = (SERVER = DEDICATED) (SERVICE_NAME =
     failover))
  )
```

4.1.1 Identities in the Credential Store

The next step is to centralize security using aliases within a credentials store. Run the following within GGSCI on the source:

```
cd $ORACLE_GG
ggsci
add credentialstore
```

and it looks like this:

```
GGSCI (bigdata.localdomain) 14> add credentialstore
Credential store created in ./dircrd/.
```

> *GoldenGate allows storage of credentials into a credential store file within the subdir structure under the credential store files directory (dircrd).*

And now add a user:

```
alter credentialstore add user ggate, password ggate, alias
extuser
```

and here is the result:

```
GGSCI (bigdata.localdomain) 15> alter credentialstore add user
ggate, password ggate, alias extuser
Credential store in ./dircrd/ altered.
```

And the result is an encrypted wallet file in the credential store directory:

```
[oracle@bigdata.localdomain oggcore_1-bigdata]$ ls dircrd
cwallet.sso
```

Also, given that only a single instance of a user name is allowed in the credential store, then it follows that multiple aliases can be created for a single user, unless the ALIAS option is used:

```
GGSCI (bigdata.localdomain) 1> alter credentialstore add user
ggate, password ggate, alias extuser2
Credential store in ./dircrd/ altered.
```

And next examine the contents of the wallet file in the credential store:

```
GGSCI (bigdata.localdomain) 2> info credentialstore
Reading from ./dircrd/:
Default domain: OracleGoldenGate
  Alias: extuser
  Userid: ggate
  Alias: extuser2
  Userid: ggate
```

Connecting with Aliases

An alias can now be used to connect to GoldenGate, as opposed to using a USERID and PASSWORD, thus exchanging this:

```
DBLOGIN USERID ggate, PASSWORD ggate
```

for this:

```
DBLOGIN USERIDALIAS extuser
```

as shown here:

```
GGSCI (bigdata.localdomain) 3> DBLOGIN USERID ggate, PASSWORD
ggate
Successfully logged into database.
GGSCI (bigdata.localdomain) 5> DBLOGIN USERIDALIAS extuser
Successfully logged into database.
```

   Next do the same on the target for the Replicat process:

```
add credentialstore
alter credentialstore add user ggate, password ggate, alias
abcuser
info credentialstore
GGSCI (failover.localdomain) 8> info credentialstore
Reading from ./dircrd/:
Default domain: OracleGoldenGate
  Alias: abcuser
  Userid: ggate
```

If an error is made, as above, then help can be found using the HELP command, as shown in Figure 4.1.

And one can then remove the error and replace with a correction as follows:

```
delete credentialstore
add credentialstore
alter credentialstore add user ggate, password ggate, alias
repuser
info credentialstore
```

and it looks like this for the Replicat process:

```
GGSCI (failover.localdomain) 13> delete credentialstore
```

```
GGSCI (failover.localdomain) 9> help

GGSCI Command Summary:

Object:          Command:
SUBDIRS          CREATE
DATASTORE        ALTER, CREATE, DELETE, INFO, REPAIR
ER               INFO, KILL, LAG, SEND, STATUS, START, STATS, STOP
EXTRACT          ADD, ALTER, CLEANUP, DELETE, INFO, KILL,
                 LAG, REGISTER, SEND, START, STATS, STATUS, STOP
                 UNREGISTER
EXTTRAIL         ADD, ALTER, DELETE, INFO
GGSEVT           VIEW
JAGENT           INFO, START, STATUS, STOP
MANAGER          INFO, SEND, START, STOP, STATUS
MARKER           INFO
PARAMETERS       EDIT, VIEW, SET EDITOR, INFO, GETPARAMINFO
REPLICAT         ADD, ALTER, CLEANUP, DELETE, INFO, KILL, LAG, REGISTER, SEND,
                 START, STATS, STATUS, STOP, SYNCHRONIZE, UNREGISTER
REPORT           VIEW
RMTTRAIL         ADD, ALTER, DELETE, INFO
TRACETABLE       ADD, DELETE, INFO
TRANDATA         ADD, DELETE, INFO
SCHEMATRANDATA   ADD, DELETE, INFO
CHECKPOINTTABLE  ADD, DELETE, CLEANUP, INFO, UPGRADE
WALLET           CREATE, OPEN, PURGE
MASTERKEY        ADD, INFO, RENEW, DELETE, UNDELETE
CREDENTIALSTORE  ADD, ALTER, INFO, DELETE
HEARTBEATTABLE   ADD, DELETE, ALTER, INFO
HEARTBEATENTRY   DELETE

Commands without an object:
(Database)       DBLOGIN, LIST TABLES, ENCRYPT PASSWORD, FLUSH SEQUENCE
                 MININGDBLOGIN, SET NAMECCSID
(DDL)            DUMPDDL
(Miscellaneous)  ! ,ALLOWNESTED | NOALLOWNESTED, CREATE SUBDIRS,
                 DEFAULTJOURNAL, FC, HELP, HISTORY, INFO ALL, OBEY, SHELL,
                 SHOW, VERSIONS, VIEW GGSEVT, VIEW REPORT
                 (note: type the word COMMAND after the ! to display the
                 ! help topic, for example: GGSCI (sys1)> help ! command

For help on a specific command, type HELP <command> <object>.

Example: HELP ADD REPLICAT
```

Figure 4.1   GGSCI Available Commands

```
ERROR: Unable to delete credential store from ./dircrd/.
GGSCI (failover.localdomain) 14> add credentialstore
Credential store created in ./dircrd/.
GGSCI (failover.localdomain) 15> alter credentialstore add
user ggate, password ggate, alias repuser
Credential store in ./dircrd/ altered.
GGSCI (failover.localdomain) 16> info credentialstore
Reading from ./dircrd/:
Default domain: OracleGoldenGate
  Alias: repuser
  Userid: ggate
```

Using Aliases in Parameter Files

The next step is to substitute the USERID entry in the source Extract process parameter file for an alias, replacing this:

```
USERID ggate@failover, PASSWORD ggate
```

with this, and thus reading the credentials into the Extract parameter file:

```
USERIDALIAS extuser
```

leaving the Extract process parameter file looking like this:

```
EXTRACT ext1
USERIDALIAS extuser
rmthost failover, mgrport 7809
rmttrail /u01/app/oracle/product/12.1.0/oggcore_1/dirdat/lt
ddl include mapped objname capture.*, include mapped objname
bigdata.*, include mapped objname email.*, include mapped
objname dmevents.*
table capture.*;
table bigdata.*;
table email.*;
table dmevents.*;
```

Next, one can also change the Replicat parameter file on the target server:

```
REPLICAT rep1
ASSUMETARGETDEFS
USERIDALIAS repuser
DISCARDFILE /u01/app/oracle/product/12.1.0/oggcore_1/dirdat/
rep1_discard.txt, APPEND, MEGABYTES 10
DDL
--Maps tables from source to target
MAP CAPTURE.*, TARGET APPLI.*;
MAP bigdata.*, TARGET bigdata.*;
MAP email.*, TARGET email.*;
MAP dmevents.*, TARGET dmevents.*;
```

The Extract process was restarted and tested, and the same can be done with the Replicat process, restarting that Replicat process and testing it:

```
GGSCI (failover.localdomain as ggate@failover) 26> stop
replicat rep1
Sending STOP request to REPLICAT REP1 ...
Request processed.

GGSCI (failover.localdomain as ggate@failover) 27> start
replicat rep1
Sending START request to MANAGER ...
REPLICAT REP1 starting

GGSCI (failover.localdomain as ggate@failover) 28> DBLOGIN
USERIDALIAS repuser
Successfully logged into database.
```

4.1.2 Password Encryption

There is more than one method of applying encryption for use with Oracle GoldenGate, where not only can database passwords be stored in encrypted form, but additionally all trail files can be sent across a network between source and target server in encrypted form. Encryption can also be stored locally on each server or centrally on a designated server. The simplest method of managing encrypted passwords is by using an encryption key stored in a local file, which can be used for password and trail encryption (trail encryption is out of the scope of this book). So in the GoldenGate home directory, generate one key using the following:

```
cd $ORACLE_GG
. /keygen 128 1
```

The above returns a single key as follows:

```
[oracle@bigdata.localdomain oggcore_1-bigdata]$ ./keygen 128 1
0xDCA1D11DFBD43D644708B62E8CA6A725
```

Now save the key in a file in the GoldenGate home directory as a file called ENCKEYS, giving the key created a unique name like this:

```
[oracle@bigdata.localdomain oggcore_1-bigdata]$ cat ENCKEYS
key1 0xDCA1D11DFBD43D644708B62E8CA6A725
```

The Extract trail on the source server can be encrypted by adding the following line to the Extract parameters file on the source, the demonstration of which is out of scope of this book:

```
ENCRYPTTRAIL AES128 KEYNAME key1
```

Encrypting a password in GoldenGate uses the ENCRYPT PASSWORD command inside GGSCI as follows:

```
ENCRYPT PASSWORD ggate AES128 ENCRYPTKEY key1
```

and the output should look like that shown below, describing an encrypted form of the password based on the encryption key created in the ENCKEYS file by using the keygen utility:

```
GGSCI (bigdata.localdomain) 2> ENCRYPT PASSWORD ggate AES128
ENCRYPTKEY key1
Encrypted password:
AADAAAAAAAAAAAFABEREACWDCIGHVGLAGGYHUGSAWAFDIFEIOIUBBEQHMILHSG
YCVCYEIISHFFXDOJNG
Algorithm used:  AES128
```

The next step is to utilize the encrypted password so that the password is not stored in plain text in a file on a machine. Examine the DBLOGIN command syntax used for connecting in GGSCI to GoldenGate, clearly showing below the use of an encrypted password:

```
DBLOGIN { [SOURCEDB data_source] | [, database@host:port] |
USERID {/ | userid}[, PASSWORD password] [algorithm ENCRYPTKEY
{keyname | DEFAULT}] | USERIDALIAS alias [DOMAIN domain] |
[SYSDBA | SQLID sqlid] [SESSIONCHARSET character_set] }
```

So essentially, one can connect in GGSCI to an Oracle user by way of a user or an alias, as well as an encrypted password:

```
DBLOGIN USERID ggate, PASSWORD AADAAAAAAAAAAAFABEREACWDCIGHVGL
AGGYHUGSAWAFDIFEIOIUBBEQHMILHSGYCVCYEIISHFFXDOJNG, AES128,
ENCRYPTKEY key1
```

and the result is a successful connection that does not expose a password, only the encrypted password:

```
GGSCI (bigdata.localdomain) 4> DBLOGIN USERID ggate, PASSWORD
AADAAAAAAAAAAAFABEREACWDCIGHVGLAGGYHUGSAWAFDIFEIOIUBBEQHMILHSG
YCVCYEIISHFFXDOJNG, AES128, ENCRYPTKEY key1
Successfully logged into database.
```

Encrypted passwords do not apply to use of aliases in the Credential Store, because the credential store is already stored in the operating system as a binary encrypted wallet file.

Placing an encrypted password into the Extract process parameter file is a simple matter of appropriately editing the Extract process parameter file on the source, and then restarting the Extract process:

```
EXTRACT ext1
```

```
USERID ggate, PASSWORD AADAAAAAAAAAAAAFABEREACWDCIGHVGLAGGYHUGS
AWAFDIFEIOIUBBEQHMILHSGYCVCYEIISHFFXDOJNG, AES128, ENCRYPTKEY
key1
rmthost failover, mgrport 7809
rmttrail /u01/app/oracle/product/12.1.0/oggcore_1/dirdat/lt
ddl include mapped objname capture.*, include mapped objname
bigdata.*, include mapped objname email.*, include mapped
objname dmevents.*
table capture.*;
table bigdata.*;
table email.*;
table dmevents.*;
```

Change the Extract process parameters file back and restart the Extract process:

```
EXTRACT ext1
USERIDALIAS extuser
rmthost failover, mgrport 7809
rmttrail /u01/app/oracle/product/12.1.0/oggcore_1/dirdat/lt
ddl include mapped objname capture.*, include mapped objname
bigdata.*, include mapped objname email.*, include mapped
objname dmevents.*
table capture.*;
table bigdata.*;
table email.*;
table dmevents.*;
```

In addition, we can remove the ENCKEYS files in the GoldenGate home directory $ORACLE_GGHOME using a command such as this:

```
[oracle@bigdata.localdomain oggcore_1-bigdata]$ rm -f ENCKEYS
```

4.2 Using the GGSCI Command Line Interface

Much of the needed information for working with GGSCI has been covered in previous chapters, but this section will fill in some of the gaps.

4.2.1 GGSCI Commands

All the commands available within the GGSCI command line interface are as shown in Table 4.1 (on next page), showing a list and application of each command type within the GGSCI command line interface.

Table 4.1 excludes a final category of miscellaneous commands, which are as shown in the list of miscellaneous commands in Table 4.2.

A reference for all GGSCI commands can be found in Chapter 1 of the Oracle GoldenGate book titled, Fusion Middleware Reference for Oracle Golden-Gate for Windows® and *NIX, at the URL: http://docs.oracle.com/goldengate/c1221/gg-winux/GWURF/summary-oracle-goldengate-commands.htm

---

Demonstrating some of these commands inside GGSCI is as shown in the commands demonstrated below, executed from inside GGSCI:

```
cd $ORACLE_GG
ggsci
```

The INFO ER * command returns information about all groups:

```
GGSCI (bigdata.localdomain) 1> info er *
EXTRACT      EXT1      Last Started 2017-04-29 14:28  Status STOPPED
Checkpoint Lag          00:00:00 (updated 199:28:33 ago)
Log Read Checkpoint  Oracle Redo Logs
                     2017-04-29 14:30:07  Seqno 284, RBA 4249600
                     SCN 0.4760913 (4760913)
```

and getting more specific about a particular group name pattern, which happens to be the only group on this source server:

```
GGSCI (bigdata.localdomain) 2> info er ext*
EXTRACT      EXT1      Last Started 2017-04-29 14:28  Status STOPPED
Checkpoint Lag          00:00:00 (updated 199:32:08 ago)
Log Read Checkpoint  Oracle Redo Logs
                     2017-04-29 14:30:07  Seqno 284, RBA 4249600
                     SCN 0.4760913 (4760913)
```

Table 4.1 GGSCI Available Commands

GGSCI Command	Description
Manager	GoldenGate parent process
Extract	Process to capture change in a source database
Replicat	Process to apply change to a target database
ER *	Issue Extract and Replicat commands to multiple Extract and Replicat groups
Wallet	Encryption and the master key wallet
Credential Store	Credential store details
Trail	Trails used to store change made to a source before being applied to a target
Parameter	Parameter files
Database	Database interaction
Trandata	Transactional-level configuration for data produced from a source database
Checkpoint Table	Tracks the position of the Replicat process within a trail
Oracle Trace Table	Tracing prevents loopback between source and target databases
Data Store	Monitoring information storage
Monitor JAgent	JAgent monitoring control
Automatic Heartbeat	Heartbeat functionality between source and target databases

Table 4.2 Miscellaneous Commands Available in the GGSCI Command Line Interface

GGSCI Command	Description
!	Run previous command
[NO]ALLOWNESTED	OBEY command file nesting
CREATE SUBDIRS	Default directory creation upon initial GoldenGate installation and configuration
FC	Change and execute the previous command
HISTORY	History of commands executed inside GGSCI
INFO ALL	Show all process status settings
INFO MARKER	Process markers display
OBEY	Group lists of commands for later re-execution
SHELL	Run shell commands inside GGSCI
SHOW	Attributes display
VERSIONS	Operating system and database versions
VIEW GGSEVT	Display the ggserrlog file
VIEW REPORT	Display discards file created by Extract and Replicat processes

Here is a SHELL command executing a Linux ls command from inside the GGSCI tool:

```
GGSCI (bigdata.localdomain) 6> shell ls -larth
total 618M
-rw-r-----  1 oracle oinstall 1.5K Oct 15  2010 zlib.txt
-rw-r-----  1 oracle oinstall  759 Oct 15  2010 tcperrs
-rw-r-----  1 oracle oinstall  248 Oct 15  2010 sqlldr.tpl
-rw-r-----  1 oracle oinstall 1.7K Oct 15  2010 libxml2.txt
...
drwxr-x---  2 oracle oinstall 4.0K Apr 29 14:28 dirrpt
drwxr-x---  2 oracle oinstall 4.0K Apr 29 14:30 dirpcs
drwxr-xr-x 27 oracle oinstall 4.0K May  7 01:29 .
-rw-r-----  1 oracle oinstall 365K May  7 22:02 ggserr.log
```

The SHOW command returns all attribute context settings inside the current instantiation of the GGSCI command:

```
GGSCI (bigdata.localdomain) 7> show

Parameter settings:
SET SUBDIRS     ON
SET DEBUG       OFF

Current directory: /u01/app/oracle/product/12.1.0/oggcore_1
Using subdirectories for all process files
Editor:  vi

Reports (.rpt)              /u01/app/oracle/product/12.1.0/
oggcore_1/dirrpt
Parameters (.prm)           /u01/app/oracle/product/12.1.0/
oggcore_1/dirprm
Replicat Checkpoints (.cpr)  /u01/app/oracle/product/12.1.0/
oggcore_1/dirchk
Extract Checkpoints (.cpe)   /u01/app/oracle/product/12.1.0/
oggcore_1/dirchk
Process Status (.pcs)       /u01/app/oracle/product/12.1.0/
oggcore_1/dirpcs
```

```
SQL Scripts (.sql)              /u01/app/oracle/product/12.1.0/
oggcore_1/dirsql
Database Definitions (.def)     /u01/app/oracle/product/12.1.0/
oggcore_1/dirdef
Dump files (.dmp)               /u01/app/oracle/product/12.1.0/
oggcore_1/dirdmp
Masterkey wallet files (.wlt)   /u01/app/oracle/product/12.1.0/
oggcore_1/dirwlt
Credential store files (.crd)   /u01/app/oracle/product/12.1.0/
oggcore_1/dircrd
```

The VERSIONS command returns the versions of the operating system and database:

```
GGSCI (bigdata.localdomain) 8> versions
Operating System:
Linux
Version #1 SMP Wed Aug 3 22:33:10 PDT 2016, Release
2.6.39-400.283.2.el5uek
Node: bigdata.localdomain
Machine: x86_64
Database:
ERROR: Not logged into database, use DBLOGIN.
```

Some of the VERSIONS command information requires a database connection within GGSCI:

```
GGSCI (bigdata.localdomain) 10> dblogin useridalias extuser
Successfully logged into database.

GGSCI (bigdata.localdomain as ggate@bigdata) 11> versions
Operating System:
Linux
Version #1 SMP Wed Aug 3 22:33:10 PDT 2016, Release
2.6.39-400.283.2.el5uek
Node: bigdata.localdomain
Machine: x86_64
Database:
```

```
Oracle Database 12c Enterprise Edition Release 12.1.0.2.0 -
64bit Production
PL/SQL Release 12.1.0.2.0 - Production
CORE    12.1.0.2.0        Production
TNS for Linux: Version 12.1.0.2.0 - Production
NLSRTL Version 12.1.0.2.0 - Production
```

4.2.2 More on the Manager Process

Inside the GGSCI tool, the Manager process can be stopped and started using the following, where MGR and MANAGER are synonymous and case is irrelevant:

```
START MANAGER
START MGR
start manager
start mgr
STOP MANAGER
STOP MGR
stop manager
stop mgr
```

Using the ! mark with the STOP MANAGER command removes the prompt:

```
GGSCI (bigdata.localdomain) 19> stop mgr
Manager process is required by other GGS processes.
Are you sure you want to stop it (y/n)?y

Sending STOP request to MANAGER ...
Request processed.
Manager stopped.
```

and with the prompt removed:

```
GGSCI (bigdata.localdomain) 20> start mgr
Manager started.

GGSCI (bigdata.localdomain) 21> stop mgr!
Sending STOP request to MANAGER ...
```

```
Request processed.
Manager stopped.
```

The Manager process can also be started in an operating system shell using the MGR command, as follows:

```
mgr paramfile /u01/app/oracle/product/12.1.0/oggcore_1/dirprm/
mgr.prm
```

> There is an optional reportfile argument that can store a report called the "Manager process report," which is normally stored in the report files (/u01/app/oracle/product/ 12.1.0/oggcore_1/dirrpt) subdirectory.

Process Parameters

The current Manager process parameters file thus far built for this book contain a single line, which is just a port, which is the default GoldenGate port for communicating between source and target databases. The Manager process parameter file can be edited using the EDIT PARAMS MGR command inside GGSCI, as well as editing the file that can be listed on screen using the cat command as shown below:

```
cat /u01/app/oracle/product/12.1.0/oggcore_1/dirprm/mgr.prm
```

and the result looks like this:

```
[oracle@bigdata.localdomain oggcore_1-bigdata]$ cat /u01/app/
oracle/product/12.1.0/oggcore_1/dirprm/mgr.prm
PORT 7809
```

In addition, there are a number of other useful Manager process parameters, as described below:

- AUTOSTART automatically starts Extract and Replicat processes when the Manager process starts. AUTORESTART does the same but only after abnormal termination.
- PURGEOLDEXTRACTS clears trails after processing is complete, without which the trail files can grow to consume too much, even perhaps all, available disk space and cause a server crash.

- STARTUPVALIDATIONONDELAY[SECS] delays validation of other processes after the Manager process has begun, such as Extract and Replicat processes.

And below is an example Manager process parameters file on the source for the Extract process:

```
PORT 7809
ACCESSRULE, PROG *, ALLOW
AUTOSTART
STARTUPVALIDATIONDELAY 2
PURGEOLDEXTRACTS /u01/app/oracle/product/12.1.0/oggcore_1/
dirdat/lt*
```

and on a target for a Replicat process:

```
PORT 7809
ACCESSRULE, PROG *, ALLOW
AUTOSTART
STARTUPVALIDATIONDELAY 2
```

The above configuration will yield an error on the source when starting the Extract process, if the Replicat process is not first started on a target.

4.2.3 More on the Extract and Replicat Processes

Sometimes when starting and stopping the Extract and Replicat processes, those processes cannot be stopped easily and can only be killed with the following syntax, but note that replicated changes could be lost:

```
kill { extract | replicat } <group-names>
```

In addition, commands can be executed using a wildcard catering to all items within a group, such as killing all processes on a server:

```
stop er *
```

or killing the processes if no response is received:

```
kill er *
```

Conversely, the following command will start up all group processes on the server concerned:

```
start extract *
```

Wildcards can also be used with other commands—for example, where the following command will start all processes named as *1, such as an Extract process called ext1 and an Extract process called anotherext1:

```
start extract *1
```

> Deleting, registering, and unregistering Extract and Replicat process groups has already been covered in a previous chapter.

4.2.4 Automation in GGSCI

Automation can be executed using the HISTORY command, as a script redirected in a shell into GGSCI, and also as a file name added as the parameter to the OBEY command within the GGSCI tool.

The GGSCI HISTORY Command

The HISTORY command can be used inside GGSCI to display and re-execute commands that have already been typed into a currently open GGSCI session, meaning that simply executing the GGSCI tool without anything started results in no command history:

```
GGSCI (bigdata.localdomain) 1> history
GGSCI Command History
    1: history
```

So some processing was executed to start the Manager on the source, start the Manager on the target, start Replicat on the target, followed by starting Extract on the source, and finally stopping everything on both source and target—so the source history is:

```
GGSCI (bigdata.localdomain) 11> history
```

```
GGSCI Command History
    2: help
    3: start mgr
    4: info all
    5: start extract ext1
    6: info all
    7: view ggsevt
    8: info all
    9: start extract ext1
   10: info all
   11: history
   12: stop ER *
   13: info all
   14: stop mgr
   15: info all
   16: history
```

and the target history is:

```
GGSCI (failover.localdomain) 4> history
GGSCI Command History
    1: start mgr
    2: start replicat rep1
    3: info all
    4: history
    5: stop ER *
    6: info all
    7: stop mgr!
    8: info all
    9: history
```

So on the source one could re-execute a previous command using the !
command on the target and pull up the history again:

```
GGSCI (failover.localdomain) 10> !9
history
GGSCI Command History
    1: start mgr
```

```
 2: start replicat rep1
 3: info all
 4: history
 5: stop ER *
 6: info all
 7: stop mgr!
 8: info all
 9: history
10: history
```

The FC command can be used to edit and re-execute that edited command—the Enter key must be hit twice when the number line 11 [GGSCI (failover.localdomain) 11..] line appears, as shown below, substituting stop mgr! with start mgr:

```
GGSCI (failover.localdomain) 11> FC 14
GGSCI (failover.localdomain) 11> stop mgr!
GGSCI (failover.localdomain) 11..start mgr
GGSCI (failover.localdomain) 11..
Manager started.

GGSCI (failover.localdomain) 22> info all
Program       Status       Group      Lag at Chkpt    Time Since Chkpt
MANAGER       RUNNING
REPLICAT      STOPPED      REP1       00:00:00        00:10:17
```

> More details on how to use the FC command can be found at the URL: https://docs.oracle.com/goldengate/1212/gg-winux/GWURF/ggsci_commands.htm#GWURF110

Automating GGSCI Commands in Scripts Using the OBEY Command

A file containing commands can be redirected into the GGSCI utility from what GoldenGate calls an OBEYfile:

```
ggsci < OBEYfile.in
```

The following OBEYfile example will stop the Extract and Manager processes on the source server using a script and return to the operating system prompt:

```
$ cat obeyextract.txt
stop extract ext1
stop mgr!
info all
```

The result is as shown below, where the stop mgr! command does not return a prompt:

```
$ ggsci < obeyextract.txt

Oracle GoldenGate Command Interpreter for Oracle
Version 12.2.0.1.1 OGGCORE_12.2.0.1.0_PLATFORMS_151211.1401_FBO
Linux, x64, 64bit (optimized), Oracle 12c on Dec 12 2015
02:56:48
Operating system character set identified as UTF-8.

Copyright (C) 1995, 2015, Oracle and/or its affiliates. All
rights reserved.

GGSCI (bigdata.localdomain) 1>
Sending STOP request to EXTRACT EXT1 ...
Request processed.

GGSCI (bigdata.localdomain) 2>
Sending STOP request to MANAGER ...
Request processed.
Manager stopped.

GGSCI (bigdata.localdomain) 3>
Program      Status      Group      Lag at Chkpt   Time Since Chkpt

MANAGER      STOPPED
EXTRACT      STOPPED     EXT1       00:00:00       00:00:03
```

The OBEY command can be used within the GGSCI tool to execute a set of commands as a script:

```
GGSCI (bigdata.localdomain) 5> OBEY obeyextract.txt

GGSCI (bigdata.localdomain) 6> stop extract ext1
Sending STOP request to EXTRACT EXT1 ...
Request processed.

GGSCI (bigdata.localdomain) 7> stop mgr!
Sending STOP request to MANAGER ...
Request processed.
Manager stopped.

GGSCI (bigdata.localdomain) 8> info all
Program      Status      Group    Lag at Chkpt   Time Since Chkpt
MANAGER      STOPPED
EXTRACT      STOPPED     EXT1     00:00:00       00:00:05
```

4.2.5 Working with Parameters and Parameter Files

Parameters and parameter files are divided up into eight separate sections:

- **GLOBALS.** Applies to an entire server and not each specific process
- **Manager.** Manages processes and resources for a server
- **Parameters.** Common to Extract and Replicat
- **Extract.** Specific to the Extract process
- **Replicat.** Specific to the Replicat process
- **Wildcard Exclusion.** Works on groups of processes
- **DEFGEN.** A file containing differences in definitions of data between source and target
- **DDL.** Control of DDL support

All of the GoldenGate parameters do not need to be listed in this book and can be referred to at this URL:

```
http://docs.oracle.com/goldengate/c1221/gg-winux/GWURF/
summary-oracle-goldengate-parameters.htm#GWURF978
```

Parameters can be viewed inside the GGSCI tool using the VIEW PARAMS <process name> file:

```
GGSCI (bigdata.localdomain) 9> view params ext1
EXTRACT ext1
USERIDALIAS extuser
rmthost failover, mgrport 7809
rmttrail /u01/app/oracle/product/12.1.0/oggcore_1/dirdat/lt
ddl include mapped objname capture.*, include mapped objname
bigdata.*, include
mapped objname email.*, include mapped objname dmevents.*
table capture.*;
table bigdata.*;
table email.*;
table dmevents.*;
```

Parameter files can also be cross-checked and verified in the operating system using the CHECKPRM utility:

```
[oracle@bigdata.localdomain oggcore_1-bigdata]$ checkprm /u01/
app/oracle/product/12.1.0/oggcore_1/dirprm/ext1.prm
2017-04-29 15:05:05  INFO    OGG-10139  Parameter file /u01/
app/oracle/product/12.1.0/oggcore_1/dirprm/ext1.prm:  Validity
check: PASS.
Runtime parameter validation is not reflected in the above
check.
```

4.3 GoldenGate Backups

The simplest method of backup for a GoldenGate installation is to back up all source and target databases, but also to include backup copies of the entire GoldenGate home directory with all GoldenGate processes not running at the time of the backup snapshot. Group all files and compress the result using a simple tar command, with compression such as that below:

```
[oracle@bigdata.localdomain oggcore_1-bigdata]$ cd /backups
[oracle@bigdata.localdomain oggcore_1-bigdata]$ tar cvfz /
backups/ggate.tar.gz $ORACLE_GG/*
```

4.4 So What's Next?

This chapter has demonstrated some basic administration and configuration of Oracle GoldenGate covering credentials, as well as the use of the GGSCI tool. This information is important to cover before proceeding further, because it is necessary to fill in some detail not covered in previous chapters. The next chapter will begin to dig into real-life scenarios utilizing GoldenGate, beginning with how to initially load the state of a current source database into a replicated target database.

Chapter 5

Loading Data into GoldenGate

The goal of this chapter is to load data from a source database into a target, and thus it makes sense to begin from scratch with both a new database as well as a cleanly deinstalled and reinstalled GoldenGate installation; instructions in Chapter 7 can be used to clean up and recreate the previously built GoldenGate installation. Two loading examples are included in this chapter, which include a cold copy of an entire database using data pump, as well as a hot copy of a single table using SQL*Loader.

5.1 Cold Copying a Database with Data Pump

The simple way to create a target database is to build it from scratch, creating a new database on the target, restoring from the source, and adding in the GoldenGate configuration on the target to initiate the replication process. Start with a full export on the source database, beginning by finding the default DATA_PUMP_DIR location as shown in Figure 5.1.

Export the application schemas on the source:

```
expdp system/password@bigdata schemas=dimensions,email,facts,
facts_events,finance directory=DATA_PUMP_DIR dumpfile=source.
dmp logfile=source.log
```

Copy the exported file to the target server into the target server DATA_PUMP_DIR:

```
scp source.dmp oracle@failover.localdomain:/u02/app/oracle/
admin/failover/dpdump/
```

Import the application schemas on the target into a cleanly installed database:

```
impdp system/***@failover schemas=
dimensions,email,facts,facts_events,finance directory=DATA_
PUMP_DIR dumpfile=source.dmp logfile=source.log
```

And now set the transaction logging on the source:

```
cd $ORACLE_GG
ggsci
DBLOGIN USERID ggate, PASSWORD ggate
ADD SCHEMATRANDATA dimensions
ADD SCHEMATRANDATA email
ADD SCHEMATRANDATA facts
ADD SCHEMATRANDATA facts_events
ADD SCHEMATRANDATA finance
```

Start up replication on both source and target, and test on the source:

```
START MGR
```

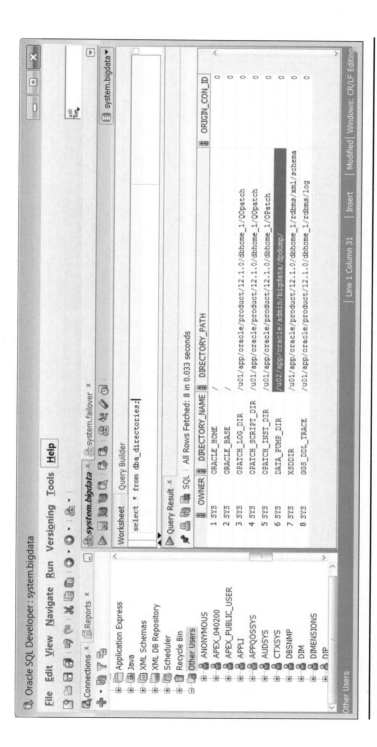

Figure 5.1 Finding the DATA_PUMP_DIR Location

```
START EXTRACT ext1
INFO ALL
```

on the target:

```
START MGR
START REPLICAT rep1
INFO ALL
```

Test on the source:

```
sqlplus facts/facts@bigdata
CREATE TABLE test(id INTEGER PRIMARY KEY);
INSERT INTO test(id) VALUES(1);
COMMIT;
```

Validate on the target:

```
sqlplus facts/facts@failover
SELECT * FROM test;
```

5.1.1 Recovering with Data Pump up to a System Change Number (SCN)

An export can be used to create a copy of data at a specific point in time using an SCN number retrieved as follows, starting on the source:

```
sqlplus / as sysdba
SQL> select current_scn from v$database;
CURRENT_SCN
-----------
    5727018
```

Next export up to the SCN using flashback, where the export will flash-back in time to an SCN, not including any changes after that SCN:

```
expdp system/****@bigdata schemas=dimensions,email,
facts,facts_events,finance directory=DATA_PUMP_DIR
```

```
dumpfile=source.flashback.dmp logfile=source.flashback.log
flashback_scn=5727018
```

Copy the file from the source to the target:

```
scp /u02/app/oracle/admin/bigdata/dpdump/source.flashback.dmp
oracle@failover:/u02/app/oracle/admin/failover/dpdump/
```

Import the same way on the target but this time creating a new schema called TMP:

```
impdp system/****@failover schemas=dimensions remap_
schema=dimensions:tmp directory=DATA_PUMP_DIR dumpfile=source.
flashback.dmp logfile=source.flashback.log
```

Now change the parameter file on the source in GGSCI:

```
ggsci
edit params ext1
```

Add the TMP schema:

```
EXTRACT ext1
USERID ggate, password ggate
rmthost failover, mgrport 7809
rmttrail /u01/app/oracle/product/12.1.0/oggcore_1/dirdat/lt
ddl include mapped objname capture.*, include mapped objname
dimensions.*, include mapped objname email.*, include mapped
objname facts.* , include mapped objname facts_events.* ,
include mapped objname finance.*
table DIMENSIONS.*;
table EMAIL.*;
table FACTS.*;
table FACTS_EVENTS.*;
table FINANCE.*;
table TMP.*;
```

and change the Replicat parameters on the target by running GGSCI:

```
ggsci
edit params rep1
```

and adding the mapping for the TMP schema:

```
REPLICAT rep1
ASSUMETARGETDEFS
USERID ggate, PASSWORD ggate
DISCARDFILE /u01/app/oracle/product/12.1.0/oggcore_1/dirdat/
rep1_discard.txt, APPEND, MEGABYTES 10
DDL
--Maps tables from source to target
MAP CAPTURE.*, TARGET APPLI.*;
MAP DIMENSIONS.*, TARGET DIMENSIONS.*;
MAP EMAIL.*, TARGET EMAIL.*;
MAP FACTS.*, TARGET FACTS.*;
MAP FACTS_EVENTS.*, TARGET FACTS_EVENTS.*;
MAP FINANCE.*, TARGET FINANCE.*;
MAP TMP.*, TARGET TMP.*;
```

and simply start up Extract on the source:

```
start mgr
start extract ext1
```

and start up Replicat on the target up to the appropriate CSN:

```
start mgr
start replicat rep1, aftercsn 5727018
```

A GoldenGate Commit Sequence Number (CSN) is the equivalent of an Oracle System Change Number (SCN).

Now clean up by dropping the TMP user and removing TMP from the Extract and Replicat parameter files.

5.2 Hot Copying a Single Table with SQL*Loader

A hot copy allows for the replication of not as yet replicated changes, down to the individual table-level, from source to target. Begin by creating a new schema on the source:

```
drop user test cascade;
create user test identified by test;
GRANT UNLIMITED TABLESPACE TO test;
create table test.testload(string1 varchar2(32));
insert into test.testload values('testing this one');
commit;
```

And next create a new schema on the target:

```
drop user test2 cascade;
create user test2 identified by test;
GRANT UNLIMITED TABLESPACE TO test2;
create table test2.testload(string1 varchar2(32));
```

Next add the following line to the target manager process parameter file on the target:

```
edit params mgr
```

and add the following line and restart the manager process:

```
ACCESSRULE, PROG *, IPADDR 10.29.102.156, ALLOW
```

Next start the manager on both source and target:

```
start mgr
```

Next on the target database:

```
grant lock any table to ggate;
```

On the source use SOURCEISTABLE to read rows from table to table:

```
add extract ext2, sourceistable
```

Add these parameters to the new Extract process ext2 on the source:

```
EXTRACT ext2
USERID ggate, password ggate
RMTHOST failover, MGRPORT 7809
RMTTASK replicat, GROUP rep2
TABLE test.*;
```

Add these parameters to the new Replicat process rep2 on the target:

```
REPLICAT rep2
USERID ggate, password ggate
BULKLOAD
ASSUMETARGETDEFS
MAP test.*, TARGET test2.*;
```

Start the Extract process on the source:

start extract ext2

Running VIEW SSGEVT, this is what appears on the source:

```
2018-03-16 00:28:07  INFO    OGG-00975  Oracle GoldenGate
Manager for Oracle, mgr.prm:  EXTRACT EXT2 starting.
2018-03-16 00:28:07  INFO    OGG-01017  Oracle GoldenGate
Capture for Oracle, ext2.prm:  Wildcard resolution set to
IMMEDIATE because SOURCEISTABLE is used.
2018-03-16 00:28:07  INFO    OGG-00992  Oracle GoldenGate
Capture for Oracle, ext2.prm:  EXTRACT EXT2 starting.
2018-03-16 00:28:07  INFO    OGG-03059  Oracle GoldenGate
Capture for Oracle, ext2.prm:  Operating system character set
identified as UTF-8.
2018-03-16 00:28:07  INFO    OGG-02695  Oracle GoldenGate
Capture for Oracle, ext2.prm:  ANSI SQL parameter syntax is
used for parameter parsing.
```

```
2018-03-16 00:28:08   INFO     OGG-03522  Oracle GoldenGate
Capture for Oracle, ext2.prm:  Setting session time zone to
source database time zone '-05:00'.
2018-03-16 00:28:08   INFO     OGG-06508  Oracle GoldenGate
Capture for Oracle, ext2.prm:  Wildcard MAP (TABLE) resolved
(entry test.*): TABLE "TEST"."TESTLOAD".
2018-03-16 00:28:08   WARNING OGG-06439  Oracle GoldenGate
Capture for Oracle, ext2.prm:  No unique key is defined for
table TESTLOAD. All viable columns will be used to represent
the key, b
ut may not guarantee uniqueness. KEYCOLS may be used to define
the key.
2018-03-16 00:28:08   INFO     OGG-06509  Oracle GoldenGate
Capture for Oracle, ext2.prm:  Using the following key columns
for source table TEST.TESTLOAD: STRING1.
2018-03-16 00:28:08   INFO     OGG-01851  Oracle GoldenGate
Capture for Oracle, ext2.prm:  filecaching started: thread ID:
139679175055680.
2018-03-16 00:28:08   INFO     OGG-01815  Oracle GoldenGate
Capture for Oracle, ext2.prm:  Virtual Memory Facilities for:
COM
     anon alloc: mmap(MAP_ANON)   anon free: munmap
     file alloc: mmap(MAP_SHARED)  file free: munmap
     target directories:
     /u01/app/oracle/product/12.1.0/oggcore_1/dirtmp.
2018-03-16 00:28:08   INFO     OGG-00993  Oracle GoldenGate
Capture for Oracle, ext2.prm:  EXTRACT EXT2 started.
2018-03-16 00:28:10   INFO     OGG-00987  Oracle GoldenGate
Command Interpreter for Oracle:  GGSCI command (oracle): info
all.
```

On the target system, find a similar trail of information showing success using the VIEW REPORT command, as follows:

```
* * * * * * * * * * * * * * * * * * * * * * * * * * * * * * * * * * * * * * * * * * * * * *
     **               Run Time Messages               **
* * * * * * * * * * * * * * * * * * * * * * * * * * * * * * * * * * * * * * * * * * * * * * *
```

```
2018-03-16 13:13:44  INFO    OGG-03522  Setting session time
zone to source database time zone '-05:00'.

2018-03-16 13:13:44  WARNING OGG-02760  ASSUMETARGETDEFS is
ignored because trail file  contains table definitions.

2018-03-16 13:13:44  INFO    OGG-06506  Wildcard MAP
resolved (entry test.*): MAP "TEST"."TESTLOAD", TARGET
test2."TESTLOAD".

2018-03-16 13:14:08  WARNING OGG-06439  No unique key is
defined for table TESTLOAD. All viable columns will be used to
represent the key, but may not guarantee uniqueness. KEY
COLS may be used to define the key.

2018-03-16 13:14:08  INFO    OGG-02756  The definition for
table TEST.TESTLOAD is obtained from the trail file.

2018-03-16 13:14:08  INFO    OGG-06511  Using following
columns in default map by name: STRING1.

2018-03-16 13:14:08  INFO    OGG-06510  Using the following
key columns for target table TEST2.TESTLOAD: STRING1.

2018-03-16 13:14:08  INFO    OGG-00178  owner = "TEST2", table
= "TESTLOAD".
```

Now that the load is completed, which is very useful for individual tables, start the Replicat process on the source:

```
start replicat rep2
info replicat rep2
```

and you should get something like this:

```
GGSCI (failover.localdomain) 32> start replicat rep2

Sending START request to MANAGER ...
```

```
REPLICAT REP2 starting

GGSCI (failover.localdomain) 33> info replicat rep2

REPLICAT    REP2      Initialized   2018-03-16 12:54    Status
STOPPED
Checkpoint Lag        00:00:00 (updated 00:30:44 ago)
Log Read Checkpoint   Not Available
Task                  SPECIALRUN

GGSCI (failover.localdomain) 34>
```

Next we can stop and remove the ext2 and rep2 processes and restart the initial ext1 and rep1 processes on the source and target servers, respectively—on the source:

```
delete extract ext2
```

and remove the parameters in the parameter file:

```
edit params ext2
```

On the target do the same:

```
delete replicat rep2
edit params rep2
```

Next remove the change from the target manager process parameter file:

```
ACCESSRULE, PROG *, IPADDR 10.29.102.156, ALLOW
```

and start the original Extract and Replicat process and test—on the target:

```
start replicat rep1
```

and on the source:

```
start extract ext1
```

And test on the source:

```
sqlplus dimensions/dimensions@bigdata
INSERT INTO test(id) VALUES(9);
Commit;
```

and on the target:

```
[oracle@failover.localdomain oggcore_1-failover]$ sqlplus
dimensions/dimensions@bigdata

SQL*Plus: Release 12.1.0.2.0 Production on Fri Mar 16 13:42:21
2018

Copyright (c) 1982, 2014, Oracle.  All rights reserved.

Last Successful login time: Fri Mar 16 2018 00:53:37 -04:00

Connected to:
Oracle Database 12c Enterprise Edition Release 12.1.0.2.0 -
64bit Production
With the Partitioning, OLAP, Advanced Analytics and Real
Application Testing options

SQL> select * from dimensions.test;

        ID
----------
         1
         2
         3
         5
         9
```

5.3 Other Load Options

There are numerous other methods of loading data from source to target in addition to export and SQL*Loader, which include the following:

- Copying and restoring a shut down cold copy of all database files.

- Using something called transportable tablespaces to copy an Oracle® database at the file level in the operating system.
- Using an RMAN backup from the source to recover on the target, and then recover up to an Oracle Database System Change Number (SCN). An SCN represents a point in time of the logging history of an Oracle database, and recovering up to an SCN writes log entries back into a restored database, then reapplies past changes to that database that are used to roll the target forward in time until the database is recovered.
- GoldenGate allows copying of data into and out of non-Oracle databases such as SQL Server, which is known as heterogeneous replication. Homogeneous replication includes the same database engine and version on both the source and target servers.

In reality, the easiest way to instantiate a target GoldenGate replicated database is to copy the source to the target in the simplest way, start up GoldenGate, and it is done. It is, however, possible to use a hot copy, leaving both the source and target databases running and applying changes to the target after the initial load of the target from a fixed-in-time copy.

Parallel processing can be used in Oracle databases to speed up loading of large amounts of data on large machines with many CPUs, where in its simplest form multiple Extract and Replicat processes can be used to parallel process multiple parallel streams of data copying from a source to a target server.

5.4 So What's Next?

This chapter has demonstrated some basic methods of loading a target database from an Oracle source to a target master-to-slave replication configuration. This information is important to cover because it allows for a simple introduction of instantiation of a target replicated database, similar to the topic of the next chapter of synchronization.

Chapter 6

Applying Replication

The goal of this chapter is to describe different ways in which GoldenGate can be applied that do not involve only replication. These applications include live reporting, standby, distribution, data warehouse consolidation, and high availability.

6.1 Using GoldenGate for Live Reporting

GoldenGate can be used to create two separate databases (source and target), updated automatically in one direction, where the target is used as the reporting database. The result is the removal of the overhead of the reporting function from the source database, freeing up resources for processing to allow the source database to perform the primary function of the business, and that primary function might not be backup or reporting. In addition, reporting can be more efficient when separated from different types of functionality on the source, particularly for a transaction process-ing database supporting a busy website. Figure 6.1 shows a simplistic view of the most basic GoldenGate applied configuration, the demonstration of which is described in previous chapters.

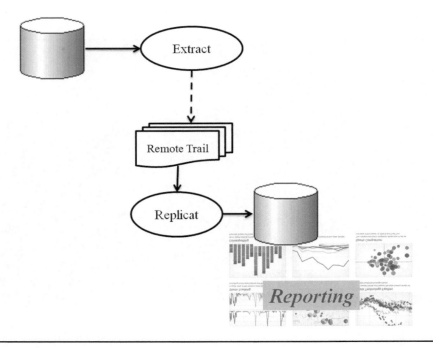

Figure 6.1   Removing Live Reporting to a GoldenGate Target

Figure 6.2 shows a live reporting connection to the source database (BIGDATA) and a reporting database, which as already stated can help to remove reporting activity from the source database, taking pressure off the primary activity of the business.

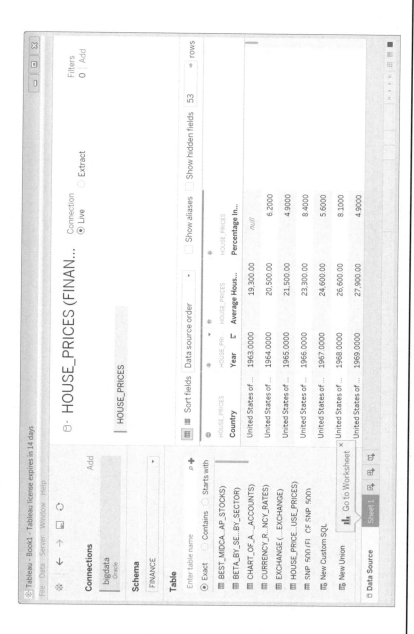

Figure 6.2 Reporting on the Source Can Overtax the Resources of the Source Database

As shown in Figure 6.3, add the target database (FAILOVER), thereby relieving the added pressure of reporting activity from the source database.

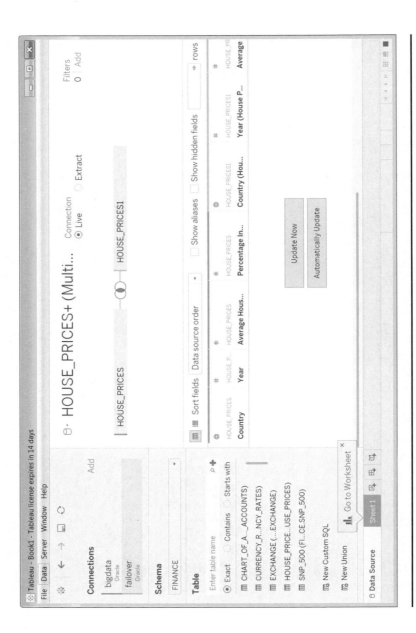

Figure 6.3   Adding the Target Database to the Reporting Tool

Figure 6.4 now removes the source connection from the reporting tool and executes a report on the target only.

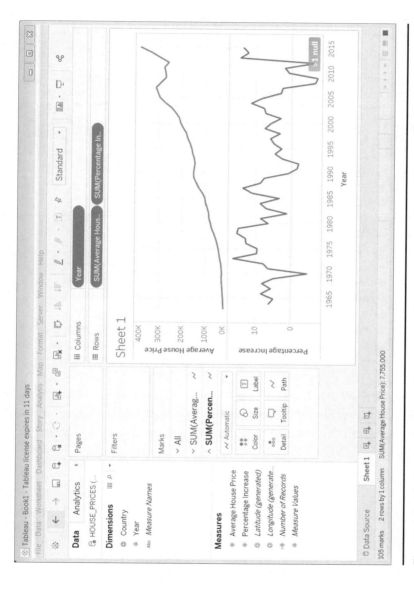

Figure 6.4 The target Database Can Execute Reports and Remove Some Processing from the Source

6.2 Using GoldenGate for a Standby/ Failover Database

The architecture of standby with GoldenGate is very simple, in that the processes from source to target are created and enabled, but the processes in reverse, from target to source, are created but disabled until a switchover (if required), as shown in Figure 6.5.

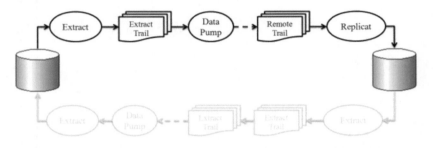

Figure 6.5   Active Standby from Source to Target

> *GoldenGate as a standby is not an automated failover. Oracle Standby (not GoldenGate) does allow an automated switchover. Oracle standby functions directly from log files, whereas GoldenGate is slower, creating trail files and possible data pump processes as additional interim steps.*

When and if there is a reason to switch source and target, then the source processes are disabled, followed by the target processes being enabled, thus reversing the source and target databases, as shown in Figure 6.6.

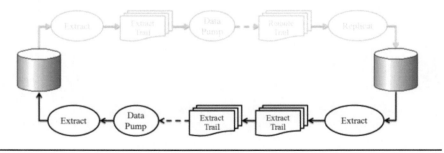

Figure 6.6   Temporary Standby from Target to Source

When the problem is resolved or source database maintenance is completed, then the best option is to switch back to the original default configuration. GoldenGate excels as a standby database option when the two databases are completely different, such as Oracle® on the source and MySQL on the target, because GoldenGate replicates at the transactional level, and even though slower than the log shipping and recovery architecture of a real standby database in Oracle Database, GoldenGate provides a simplicity and versatility that physical copying using Oracle Standby simply cannot match.

6.2.1 Implementing Standby for Two Oracle Databases Using GoldenGate

The first thing to do is to make sure that the manager is running on both source and target, as well as the Extract on the source and Replicat on the target. So on the source:

```
GGSCI (bigdata.localdomain) 4> info all
Program     Status     Group     Lag at Chkpt   Time Since Chkpt


MANAGER     RUNNING
EXTRACT     RUNNING    EXT1      00:00:00       75:37:54
```

and on the target:

```
GGSCI (failover.localdomain) 3> info all
Program     Status     Group     Lag at Chkpt   Time Since Chkpt


MANAGER     RUNNING
REPLICAT    RUNNING    REP1      00:00:00       00:00:01
```

And let's test replication from source to target. So on the source in SQLPLUS:

```
SQL> INSERT INTO test(id) VALUES(99);
1 row created.

SQL> commit;
Commit complete.
```

and on the target:

```
SQL> select * from test;

        ID
----------
         1
         2
         3
         5
         9
        99

6 rows selected.
```

Next we must configure the target, but without turning it on, beginning with schema-level logging:

```
cd $ORACLE_GG
ggsci
DBLOGIN USERID ggate, PASSWORD ggate
ADD SCHEMATRANDATA dimensions
ADD SCHEMATRANDATA email
ADD SCHEMATRANDATA facts
ADD SCHEMATRANDATA facts_events
ADD SCHEMATRANDATA finance
```

Execute these procedures on the target:

```
sqlplus / as sysdba
@marker_setup.sql
@ddl_setup.sql
@role_setup.sql
grant GGS_GGSUSER_ROLE to ggate;
@ddl_enable.sql
```

Create the Extract process on the target, the extract trail on the target, link it into the Extract process, and finally edit (create) the extract parameters on the target:

```
ADD EXTRACT ext2, TRANLOG, BEGIN NOW
ADD EXTTRAIL /u01/app/oracle/product/12.1.0/oggcore_1/dirdat/
lt, EXTRACT ext2
EDIT PARAMS ext2
```

This is the content of the ext2 extract parameters file on the target:

```
EXTRACT ext2
USERID ggate, password ggate
rmthost failover, mgrport 7809
rmttrail /u01/app/oracle/product/12.1.0/oggcore_1/dirdat/lt
ddl include mapped objname dimensions.*, include mapped
objname email.*, include mapped objname facts.* , include
mapped objname facts_events.* , include mapped objname
finance.*
table DIMENSIONS.*;
table EMAIL.*;
table FACTS.*;
table FACTS_EVENTS.*;
table FINANCE.*;
```

Create the checkpoint table on the source in the global parameters file:

```
ggsci
EDIT PARAMS ./GLOBAL
```

And add these lines to the ./GLOBAL parameters file on the source:

```
GGSCHEMA ggate
CHECKPOINTTABLE ggate.CHECKPOINT
```

Connect as the GGATE user on the source:

```
DBLOGIN USERID ggate, PASSWORD ggate
ADD CHECKPOINTTABLE ggate.CHECKPOINT
```

Next add the Replicat group on the source and link between the extract trail and the checkpoint table:

```
ADD REPLICAT rep2, EXTTRAIL /u01/app/oracle/product/12.1.0/
oggcore_1/dirdat/lt, CHECKPOINTTABLE ggate.CHECKPOINT
```

Edit the Replicat parameters file on the source:

```
EDIT PARAMS rep2
```

Add these parameters to the Replicat parameters file on the source:

```
REPLICAT rep2
ASSUMETARGETDEFS
USERID ggate, PASSWORD ggate
DISCARDFILE /u01/app/oracle/product/12.1.0/oggcore_1/dirdat/
rep1_discard.txt, APPEND, MEGABYTES 10
DDL
--Maps tables from source to target
MAP DIMENSIONS.*, TARGET DIMENSIONS.*;
MAP EMAIL.*, TARGET EMAIL.*;
MAP FACTS.*, TARGET FACTS.*;
MAP FACTS_EVENTS.*, TARGET FACTS_EVENTS.*;
MAP FINANCE.*, TARGET FINANCE.*;
```

So we now have this on the source:

```
GGSCI (bigdata.localdomain as ggate@bigdata) 6> info all
Program     Status     Group     Lag at Chkpt   Time Since Chkpt

MANAGER     RUNNING
EXTRACT     RUNNING    EXT1      00:00:00       00:00:03
REPLICAT    STOPPED    REP2      00:00:00       00:01:52
```

and this on the target:

```
GGSCI (failover.localdomain) 3> info all
Program     Status     Group     Lag at Chkpt   Time Since Chkpt

MANAGER     RUNNING
EXTRACT     STOPPED    EXT2      00:00:00       00:04:59
REPLICAT    RUNNING    REP1      00:00:00       00:00:00
```

Let's make sure that the original source-to-target replication still works. So on the source:

```
SQL> insert into test(id) values(101);
1 row created.

SQL> commit;
Commit complete.
```

and the new row appears on the target:

```
SQL> select * from test;
        ID
----------
         1
         2
         3
         5
         9
        99
       101

7 rows selected.
```

Now let's make the switchover in the following sequence beginning with the source:

```
STOP EXTRACT ext1
```

On the target:

```
STOP REPLICAT rep1
```

On the source:

```
START REPLICAT rep2
```

On the target:

```
START EXTRACT ext2
```

The source should now look like this:

```
GGSCI (bigdata.localdomain) 6> info all
Program      Status      Group      Lag at Chkpt   Time Since Chkpt

MANAGER      RUNNING
EXTRACT      STOPPED     EXT1       00:00:00       00:00:40
REPLICAT     RUNNING     REP2       00:00:00       00:00:08
```

and the target should now look like this:

```
GGSCI (failover.localdomain) 3> info all
Program      Status      Group      Lag at Chkpt   Time Since Chkpt

MANAGER      RUNNING
EXTRACT      RUNNING     EXT2       00:00:00       00:15:35
REPLICAT     STOPPED     REP1       00:00:00       00:00:35
```

And the target is now the primary:

```
SQL> insert into test(id) values(102);
1 row created.

SQL> commit;
Commit complete.
```

with the source being the secondary:

```
SQL> select * from test;

        ID
----------
         1
         2
         3
         5
         9
        99
       101
       102
```

```
8 rows selected.
```

The process can be reversed by stopping the ext2 and rep2 processes and by restarting the ext1 and rep1 processes. We can then run these on the target in SQLPLUS:

```
@ddl_disable.sql;
@ddl_remove.sql;
@marker_remove.sql;
```

And in GGSCI on the target:

```
DBLOGIN USERID ggate, PASSWORD ggate
DELETE SCHEMATRANDATA dimensions
DELETE SCHEMATRANDATA email
DELETE SCHEMATRANDATA facts
DELETE SCHEMATRANDATA facts_events
DELETE SCHEMATRANDATA finance
```

On the target:

```
DELETE EXTRACT ext2
UNREGISTER EXTRACT ext2 DATABASE
```

On the source:

```
DELETE REPLICAT rep2
UNREGISTER REPLICAT rep2 DATABASE
```

And finally restart ext1 on the source and rep1 on the target, and then test on the source:

```
SQL> insert into test(id) values(105);
1 row created.

SQL> commit;
Commit complete.
```

and on the target:

```
SQL> select * from test;

        ID
----------
         1
         2
         3
         5
         9
        99
       101
       102
       105

9 rows selected.
```

That is a clear demonstration of a standby database implementation using Oracle GoldenGate.

6.3 Using GoldenGate for Data Distribution to Many Targets

Distribution can be configured to execute replication from a single source database to two or more other master-to-slave replications. Distribution can be used to (1) spread data to multiple locations for ease of access, (2) localized performance, (3) backup copies, (4) for reporting, or (5) even to allow for network or hardware failure onto one of the targets, or (6) even a combination of all of these. Figure 6.7 shows a basic structure in which a single source database of replicating changes sends changes from one source and on to three separate target databases all at the same time.

6.3.1 Implementing Data Distribution to Two Targets

So begin with the source machine:

```
GGSCI (bigdata.localdomain) 6> info all
Program     Status     Group     Lag at Chkpt   Time Since Chkpt
```

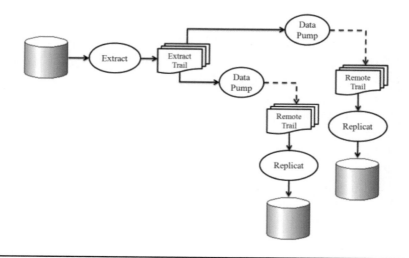

Figure 6.7   Distributing Data from a Single Source to Two or More Targets

```
MANAGER      RUNNING
EXTRACT      RUNNING    EXT1        00:00:00        38:47:44
```

Next we need to add two data pumps on the source, where each data pump talks to each separate target:

```
ADD EXTRACT pump1, EXTTRAILSOURCE /u01/app/oracle/
product/12.1.0/oggcore_1/dirdat/l1, BEGIN NOW
ADD EXTRACT pump2, EXTTRAILSOURCE /u01/app/oracle/
product/12.1.0/oggcore_1/dirdat/l2, BEGIN NOW
```

Next create two remote trails on the source, again one for each target:

```
ADD RMTTRAIL /u01/app/oracle/product/12.1.0/oggcore_1/dirdat/
l1, EXTRACT pump1
ADD RMTTRAIL /u01/app/oracle/product/12.1.0/oggcore_1/dirdat/
l2, EXTRACT pump2
```

Next create the parameter files for each data pump process on the source using the EDIT PARAMS command, beginning with the first data pump process:

```
EXTRACT pump1
USERID ggate, password ggate
RMTHOST bigdatavm1, MGRPORT 7809
RMTTRAIL /u01/app/oracle/product/12.1.0/oggcore_1/dirdat/l1
ddl include mapped objname capture.*, include mapped objname
dimensions.*, include mapped objname email.*, include mapped
objname facts.* , include mapped objname facts_events.* ,
include mapped objname finance.*
table DIMENSIONS.*;
table EMAIL.*;
table FACTS.*;
table FACTS_EVENTS.*;
table FINANCE.*;
```

and for the second data pump process:

```
EXTRACT pump2
USERID ggate, password ggate
RMTHOST bigdatavm2, MGRPORT 7809
RMTTRAIL /u01/app/oracle/product/12.1.0/oggcore_1/dirdat/l2
ddl include mapped objname capture.*, include mapped objname
dimensions.*, include mapped objname email.*, include mapped
objname facts.* , include mapped objname facts_events.* ,
include mapped objname finance.*
table DIMENSIONS.*;
table EMAIL.*;
table FACTS.*;
table FACTS_EVENTS.*;
table FINANCE.*;
```

Next comment out all the commands in the Extract process that have been moved to the data pump processes:

```
EXTRACT ext1
USERID ggate, password ggate
--rmthost failover, mgrport 7809
--rmttrail /u01/app/oracle/product/12.1.0/oggcore_1/dirdat/lt
--ddl include mapped objname capture.*, include mapped objname
dimensions.*, include mapped objname email.*, include mapped
```

```
objname facts.* , include mapped objname facts_events.* ,
include mapped objname finance.*
--table DIMENSIONS.*;
--table EMAIL.*;
--table FACTS.*;
--table FACTS_EVENTS.*;
--table FINANCE.*;
```

Now create checkpoint tables on each target beginning with the global parameters files:

```
ggsci
EDIT PARAMS ./GLOBAL
```

and add these lines to the ./GLOBAL parameters files on each target:

```
GGSCHEMA ggate
CHECKPOINTTABLE ggate.CHECKPOINT
```

And next connect as the GGATE user in GGSCI on each target and add the checkpoint table to each target:

```
DBLOGIN USERID ggate, PASSWORD ggate
ADD CHECKPOINTTABLE ggate.CHECKPOINT
```

Next add the Replicat group on each target and link between the appropriate extract trail on the source and the appropriate checkpoint table on the target. In this case, the CHECKPOINT tables are named the same on both targets, beginning with the first target:

```
ADD REPLICAT rep1, EXTTRAIL /u01/app/oracle/product/12.1.0/
oggcore_1/dirdat/l1, CHECKPOINTTABLE ggate.CHECKPOINT
```

and on the second target:

```
ADD REPLICAT rep2, EXTTRAIL /u01/app/oracle/product/12.1.0/
oggcore_1/dirdat/l2, CHECKPOINTTABLE ggate.CHECKPOINT
```

Now we have to edit the Replicat process parameters on each target server using the EDIT PARAMS command inside GGSCI. Beginning on the first target:

```
REPLICAT rep1
ASSUMETARGETDEFS
USERID ggate, PASSWORD ggate
DISCARDFILE /u01/app/oracle/product/12.1.0/oggcore_1/dirdat/
rep1_discard.txt,APPEND,MEGABYTES 10
DDL
--Maps tables from source to target
MAP DIMENSIONS.*, TARGET DIMENSIONS.*;
MAP EMAIL.*, TARGET EMAIL.*;
MAP FACTS.*, TARGET FACTS.*;
MAP FACTS_EVENTS.*, TARGET FACTS_EVENTS.*;
MAP FINANCE.*, TARGET FINANCE.*;
```

and on the second target:

```
REPLICAT rep2
ASSUMETARGETDEFS
USERID ggate, PASSWORD ggate
DISCARDFILE /u01/app/oracle/product/12.1.0/oggcore_1/dirdat/
rep2_discard.txt,APPEND,MEGABYTES 10
DDL
--Maps tables from source to target
MAP DIMENSIONS.*, TARGET DIMENSIONS.*;
MAP EMAIL.*, TARGET EMAIL.*;
MAP FACTS.*, TARGET FACTS.*;
MAP FACTS_EVENTS.*, TARGET FACTS_EVENTS.*;
MAP FINANCE.*, TARGET FINANCE.*;
```

And now to start it all up and test it in this sequence, begin with the first target:

```
START MGR
START REPLICAT rep1
```

the second target:

```
START MGR
START REPLICAT rep2
```

and on the source:

```
START MGR
START EXTRACT pump1
START EXTRACT pump2
START EXTRACT ext1
```

The source will look like this:

```
GGSCI (bigdata.localdomain) 19> info all
Program     Status      Group      Lag at Chkpt   Time Since Chkpt


MANAGER     RUNNING
EXTRACT     RUNNING     EXT1       00:00:00       00:00:04
EXTRACT     RUNNING     PUMP1      00:00:00       00:00:02
EXTRACT     RUNNING     PUMP2      00:00:00       00:00:01
```

The first target will look like this:

```
GGSCI (bigdatavm1.localdomain as ggate@vmdb1) 14> info all
Program     Status      Group      Lag at Chkpt   Time Since Chkpt


MANAGER     RUNNING
REPLICAT    RUNNING     REP1       00:00:00       00:00:08
```

and the second target will look like this:

```
GGSCI (bigdatavm2.localdomain as ggate@vmdb2) 12> info all
Program     Status      Group      Lag at Chkpt   Time Since Chkpt


MANAGER     RUNNING
REPLICAT    RUNNING     REP2       00:00:00       00:00:00
```

And now test and run on the source in SQLPLUS, as shown in Figure 6.8, and on the first target, as shown in Figure 6.9, and on the second target, as shown in Figure 6.10.

The last step would be to clean up the previous additional configuration and set everything back to the original master-to-slave GoldenGate configuration, beginning with the source:

[text continues on page 129]

```
oracle@bigdata:~

[oracle@bigdata.localdomain ~bigdata]$ sqlplus finance/finance@bigdata

SQL*Plus: Release 12.1.0.2.0 Production on Wed Apr 25 17:30:31 2018

Copyright (c) 1982, 2014, Oracle.  All rights reserved.

Last Successful login time: Wed Apr 25 2018 17:29:57 -04:00

Connected to:
Oracle Database 12c Enterprise Edition Release 12.1.0.2.0 - 64bit Production
With the Partitioning, OLAP, Advanced Analytics and Real Application Testing options

SQL> create table test1(id integer);
insert into test1(id) values(901);
commit;

Table created.

SQL>
1 row created.

SQL>
Commit complete.

SQL>
```

Figure 6.8   Distributing Data from a Single Source to Two or More Targets—Testing on the Source

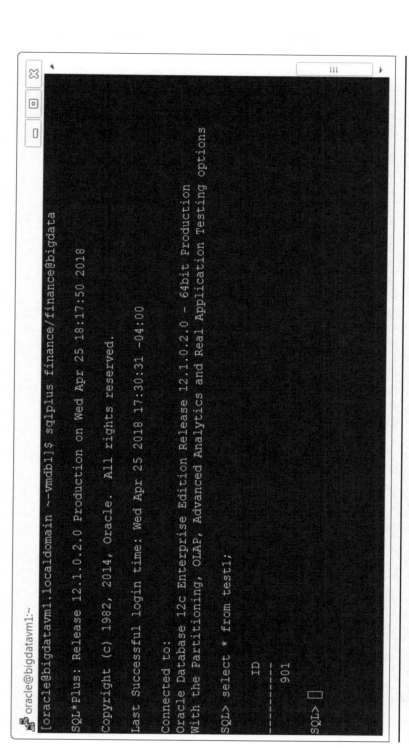

```
oracle@bigdatavm1:~

[oracle@bigdatavm1.localdomain ~vmdb1]$ sqlplus finance/finance@bigdata

SQL*Plus: Release 12.1.0.2.0 Production on Wed Apr 25 18:17:50 2018

Copyright (c) 1982, 2014, Oracle.  All rights reserved.

Last Successful login time: Wed Apr 25 2018 17:30:31 -04:00

Connected to:
Oracle Database 12c Enterprise Edition Release 12.1.0.2.0 - 64bit Production
With the Partitioning, OLAP, Advanced Analytics and Real Application Testing options

SQL> select * from test1;

        ID
----------
       901

SQL>
```

Figure 6.9 Distributing Data from a Single Source to Two or More Targets—Testing the First Target

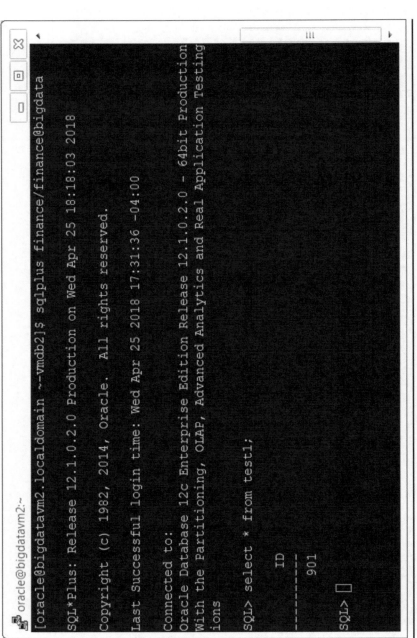

Figure 6.10 Distributing Data from a Single Source to two or More Targets—Testing the Second Target

```
GGSCI (bigdata.localdomain) 11> info all

Program      Status     Group      Lag at Chkpt  Time Since Chkpt

MANAGER      RUNNING
EXTRACT      STOPPED    EXT1       00:00:00      00:00:23
EXTRACT      ABENDED    PUMP1      00:00:00      16:18:07
EXTRACT      ABENDED    PUMP2      00:00:00      16:18:16

GGSCI (bigdata.localdomain) 12> delete extract pump1
Deleted EXTRACT PUMP1.

GGSCI (bigdata.localdomain) 13> delete extract pump2
Deleted EXTRACT PUMP2.
```

Parameters are edited and removed for the two data pump extracts, and previously added comments are removed for the ext1 Extract process:

```
GGSCI (bigdata.localdomain) 14> edit params pump1
GGSCI (bigdata.localdomain) 15> edit params pump2
GGSCI (bigdata.localdomain) 16> edit params ext1
GGSCI (bigdata.localdomain) 17>
```

Finally, we remove the Replicat processes and their associated parameters from the two target servers like this:

```
GGSCI (bigdatavm1.localdomain) 1> info all

Program      Status     Group      Lag at Chkpt  Time Since Chkpt

MANAGER      STOPPED
REPLICAT     ABENDED    REP2       00:00:00      16:48:22

GGSCI (bigdatavm1.localdomain) 2> DBLOGIN USERID ggate,
PASSWORD ggate
Successfully logged into database.
```

```
GGSCI (bigdatavm1.localdomain as ggate@vmdb2) 3> delete
replicat rep1
Deleted REPLICAT REP2.

GGSCI (bigdatavm1.localdomain as ggate@vmdb2) 4> edit params rep1
```

It is also prudent to restart all three databases to clear out any lingering GoldenGate processing.

6.4 Using GoldenGate to Consolidate a Warehouse from Many Sources

Consolidating data from multiple sources on to a single target is the general architecture that is commonly used to move data from multiple sources of information into a single target database that allows for analysis and reporting as a data warehouse. A typical data warehouse architecture using GoldenGate is as shown in Figure 6.11.

6.4.1 Implementing Data Warehouse Consolidation with GoldenGate

In this case, there are three separate source servers that will pump data changes across a network, which will be consolidated into a single target data warehouse server. Typically, a data warehouse will process and load data from one of many data sources, sometimes disparate data sources, including any kind of database such as Oracle, SQL Server, Hadoop, or even text files or other documents. The first step is to create an Extract process on all three sources and then change the parameters appropriately, applying schema-level logging:

```
cd $ORACLE_GG
ggsci
DBLOGIN USERID ggate, PASSWORD ggate
ADD SCHEMATRANDATA dimensions
ADD SCHEMATRANDATA email
ADD SCHEMATRANDATA facts
ADD SCHEMATRANDATA facts_events
ADD SCHEMATRANDATA finance
```

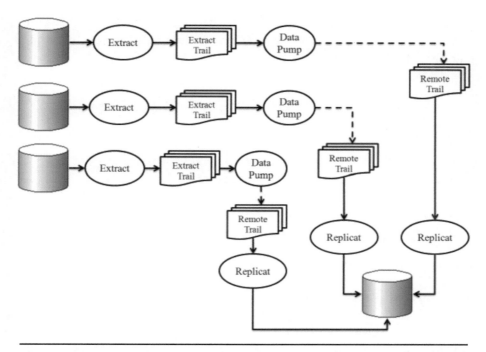

Figure 6.11   Consolidating from Multiple Sources into a Single Data Warehouse

Next run scripts to support DDL processing, adding the GGATE schema name where prompted:

```
cd $ORACLE_GG
sqlplus / as sysdba
@marker_setup.sql
@ddl_setup.sql
@role_setup.sql
grant GGS_GGSUSER_ROLE to ggate;
@ddl_enable.sql
```

Start the manager process on all three sources if not already started:

```
ggsci
info all
START MANAGER
```

On all three sources, create an Extract process, an extract trail linking into each Extract process, and edit the extract parameters on each source, starting with the first source:

```
ADD EXTRACT ext1, TRANLOG, BEGIN NOW
ADD EXTTRAIL /u01/app/oracle/product/12.1.0/oggcore_1/dirdat/
11, EXTRACT ext1
EDIT PARAMS ext1
```

And edit the parameters on the first source:

```
EXTRACT ext1
USERID ggate, password ggate
```

and on the second source:

```
ADD EXTRACT ext2, TRANLOG, BEGIN NOW
ADD EXTTRAIL /u01/app/oracle/product/12.1.0/oggcore_1/dirdat/
12, EXTRACT ext2
EDIT PARAMS ext2
```

And edit the parameters on the second source:

```
EXTRACT ext2
USERID ggate, password ggate
```

And make these changes on the third source:

```
ADD EXTRACT ext3, TRANLOG, BEGIN NOW
ADD EXTTRAIL /u01/app/oracle/product/12.1.0/oggcore_1/dirdat/
13, EXTRACT ext3
EDIT PARAMS ext3
```

And edit the parameters on the third source:

```
EXTRACT ext3
USERID ggate, password ggate
```

Next add one data pump on all three sources:

```
ADD EXTRACT pump1, EXTTRAILSOURCE /u01/app/oracle/
product/12.1.0/oggcore_1/dirdat/l1, BEGIN NOW
ADD EXTRACT pump2, EXTTRAILSOURCE /u01/app/oracle/
product/12.1.0/oggcore_1/dirdat/l2, BEGIN NOW
ADD EXTRACT pump3, EXTTRAILSOURCE /u01/app/oracle/
product/12.1.0/oggcore_1/dirdat/l3, BEGIN NOW
```

and create three remote trails, one on each source:

```
ADD RMTTRAIL /u01/app/oracle/product/12.1.0/oggcore_1/dirdat/
l1, EXTRACT pump1
ADD RMTTRAIL /u01/app/oracle/product/12.1.0/oggcore_1/dirdat/
l2, EXTRACT pump2
ADD RMTTRAIL /u01/app/oracle/product/12.1.0/oggcore_1/dirdat/
l3, EXTRACT pump3
```

Next create the parameter files for each data pump process on each source using the EDIT PARAMS command, beginning with the first data pump process on the first source:

```
EXTRACT pump1
USERID ggate, password ggate
RMTHOST bigdatavm1, MGRPORT 7809
RMTTRAIL /u01/app/oracle/product/12.1.0/oggcore_1/dirdat/l1
ddl include mapped objname capture.*, include mapped objname
dimensions.*, include mapped objname email.*, include mapped
objname facts.* , include mapped objname facts_events.* ,
include mapped objname finance.*
table DIMENSIONS.*;
table EMAIL.*;
table FACTS.*;
table FACTS_EVENTS.*;
table FINANCE.*;
```

and for the second data pump process on the second source:

```
EXTRACT pump2
USERID ggate, password ggate
RMTHOST bigdatavm2, MGRPORT 7809
```

```
RMTTRAIL /u01/app/oracle/product/12.1.0/oggcore_1/dirdat/l2
ddl include mapped objname capture.*, include mapped objname
dimensions.*, include mapped objname email.*, include mapped
objname facts.* , include mapped objname facts_events.* ,
include mapped objname finance.*
table DIMENSIONS.*;
table EMAIL.*;
table FACTS.*;
table FACTS_EVENTS.*;
table FINANCE.*;
```

and for the third data pump process on the third source:

```
EXTRACT pump3
USERID ggate, password ggate
RMTHOST bigdatavm2, MGRPORT 7809
RMTTRAIL /u01/app/oracle/product/12.1.0/oggcore_1/dirdat/l3
ddl include mapped objname capture.*, include mapped objname
dimensions.*, include mapped objname email.*, include mapped
objname facts.* , include mapped objname facts_events.* ,
include mapped objname finance.*
table DIMENSIONS.*;
table EMAIL.*;
table FACTS.*;
table FACTS_EVENTS.*;
table FINANCE.*;
```

Moving to the target, we create a checkpoint table beginning by editing the global parameters file:

```
ggsci
EDIT PARAMS ./GLOBAL
```

and add these lines to the ./GLOBAL parameters files on each target (if not already edited):

```
GGSCHEMA ggate
CHECKPOINTTABLE ggate.CHECKPOINT
```

And next connect as the GGATE user in GGSCI on the target and add the checkpoint table (if not already created):

```
DBLOGIN USERID ggate, PASSWORD ggate
ADD CHECKPOINTTABLE ggate.CHECKPOINT
```

Next we add the three Replicat groups for each source onto the target and link between the appropriate extract trail on the sources and the single checkpoint table on the target:

```
ADD REPLICAT rep1, EXTTRAIL /u01/app/oracle/product/12.1.0/
oggcore_1/dirdat/l1, CHECKPOINTTABLE ggate.CHECKPOINT
ADD REPLICAT rep2, EXTTRAIL /u01/app/oracle/product/12.1.0/
oggcore_1/dirdat/l2, CHECKPOINTTABLE ggate.CHECKPOINT
ADD REPLICAT rep3, EXTTRAIL /u01/app/oracle/product/12.1.0/
oggcore_1/dirdat/l3, CHECKPOINTTABLE ggate.CHECKPOINT
```

Now we have to edit the three Replicat process parameters on the source server using the EDIT PARAMS command inside GGSCI:

```
REPLICAT rep1
ASSUMETARGETDEFS
USERID ggate, PASSWORD ggate
DISCARDFILE /u01/app/oracle/product/12.1.0/oggcore_1/dirdat/
rep1_discard.txt,APPEND,MEGABYTES 10
DDL
--Maps tables from source to target
MAP DIMENSIONS.*, TARGET DIMENSIONS.*;
MAP EMAIL.*, TARGET EMAIL.*;
MAP FACTS.*, TARGET FACTS.*;
MAP FACTS_EVENTS.*, TARGET FACTS_EVENTS.*;
MAP FINANCE.*, TARGET FINANCE.*;
```

For the second Replicat process on the source:

```
REPLICAT rep2
ASSUMETARGETDEFS
USERID ggate, PASSWORD ggate
```

```
DISCARDFILE /u01/app/oracle/product/12.1.0/oggcore_1/dirdat/
rep1_discard.txt,APPEND,MEGABYTES 10
DDL
--Maps tables from source to target
MAP DIMENSIONS.*, TARGET DIMENSIONS.*;
MAP EMAIL.*, TARGET EMAIL.*;
MAP FACTS.*, TARGET FACTS.*;
MAP FACTS_EVENTS.*, TARGET FACTS_EVENTS.*;
MAP FINANCE.*, TARGET FINANCE.*;
```

and for the third Replicat process on the source:

```
REPLICAT rep3
ASSUMETARGETDEFS
USERID ggate, PASSWORD ggate
DISCARDFILE /u01/app/oracle/product/12.1.0/oggcore_1/dirdat/
rep1_discard.txt,APPEND,MEGABYTES 10
DDL
--Maps tables from source to target
MAP DIMENSIONS.*, TARGET DIMENSIONS.*;
MAP EMAIL.*, TARGET EMAIL.*;
MAP FACTS.*, TARGET FACTS.*;
MAP FACTS_EVENTS.*, TARGET FACTS_EVENTS.*;
MAP FINANCE.*, TARGET FINANCE.*;
```

The result should look like that as shown in Figure 6.12, with all three Replicat processes running.

And now start it all up and test it in this sequence, starting with the first target:

```
START MGR
START EXTRACT pump1
START EXTRACT ext1
```

The result should look as shown in Figure 6.13 for all three source servers.

And now we can test the GoldenGate data warehouse configuration that we have configured, starting with the first source:

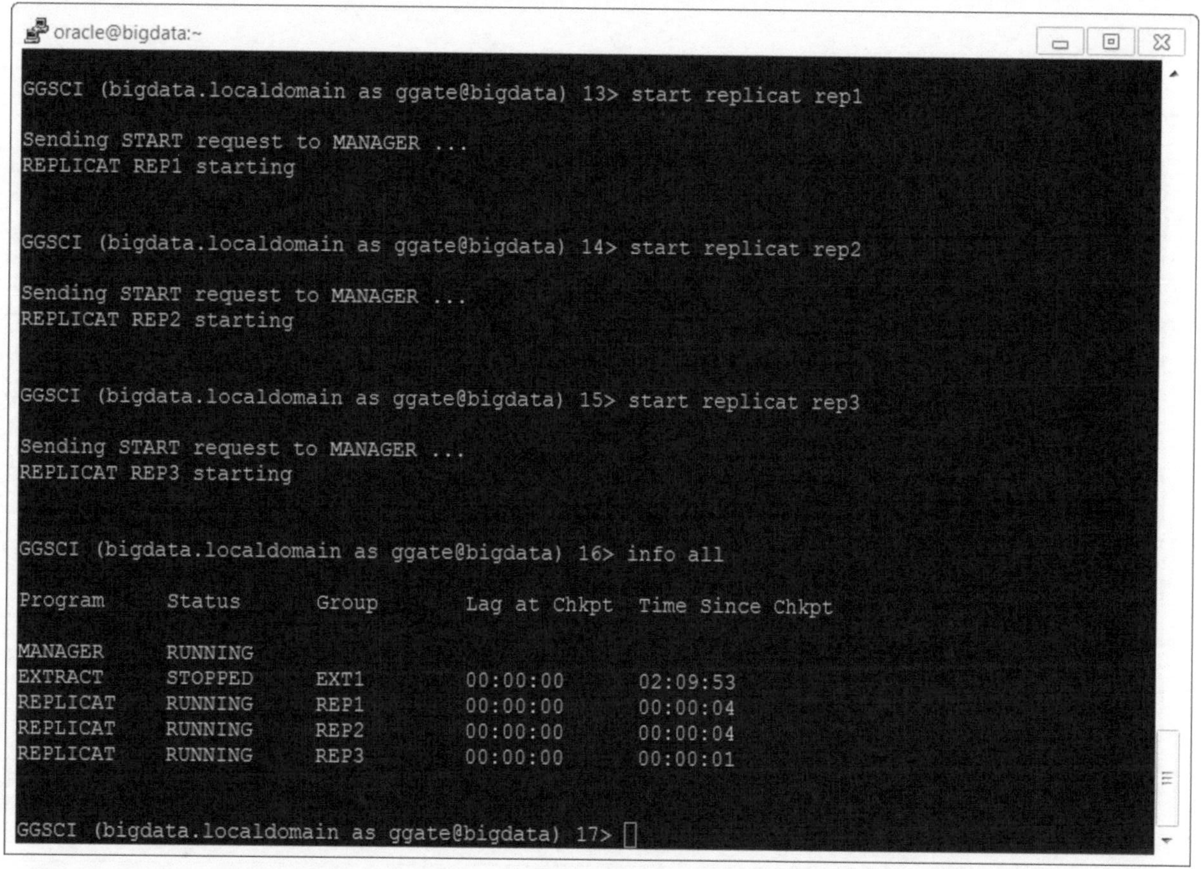

```
oracle@bigdata:~

GGSCI (bigdata.localdomain as ggate@bigdata) 13> start replicat rep1

Sending START request to MANAGER ...
REPLICAT REP1 starting

GGSCI (bigdata.localdomain as ggate@bigdata) 14> start replicat rep2

Sending START request to MANAGER ...
REPLICAT REP2 starting

GGSCI (bigdata.localdomain as ggate@bigdata) 15> start replicat rep3

Sending START request to MANAGER ...
REPLICAT REP3 starting

GGSCI (bigdata.localdomain as ggate@bigdata) 16> info all

Program     Status      Group       Lag at Chkpt  Time Since Chkpt

MANAGER     RUNNING
EXTRACT     STOPPED     EXT1        00:00:00      02:09:53
REPLICAT    RUNNING     REP1        00:00:00      00:00:04
REPLICAT    RUNNING     REP2        00:00:00      00:00:04
REPLICAT    RUNNING     REP3        00:00:00      00:00:01

GGSCI (bigdata.localdomain as ggate@bigdata) 17>
```

Figure 6.12   Starting All Three Replicat Processes on the Source

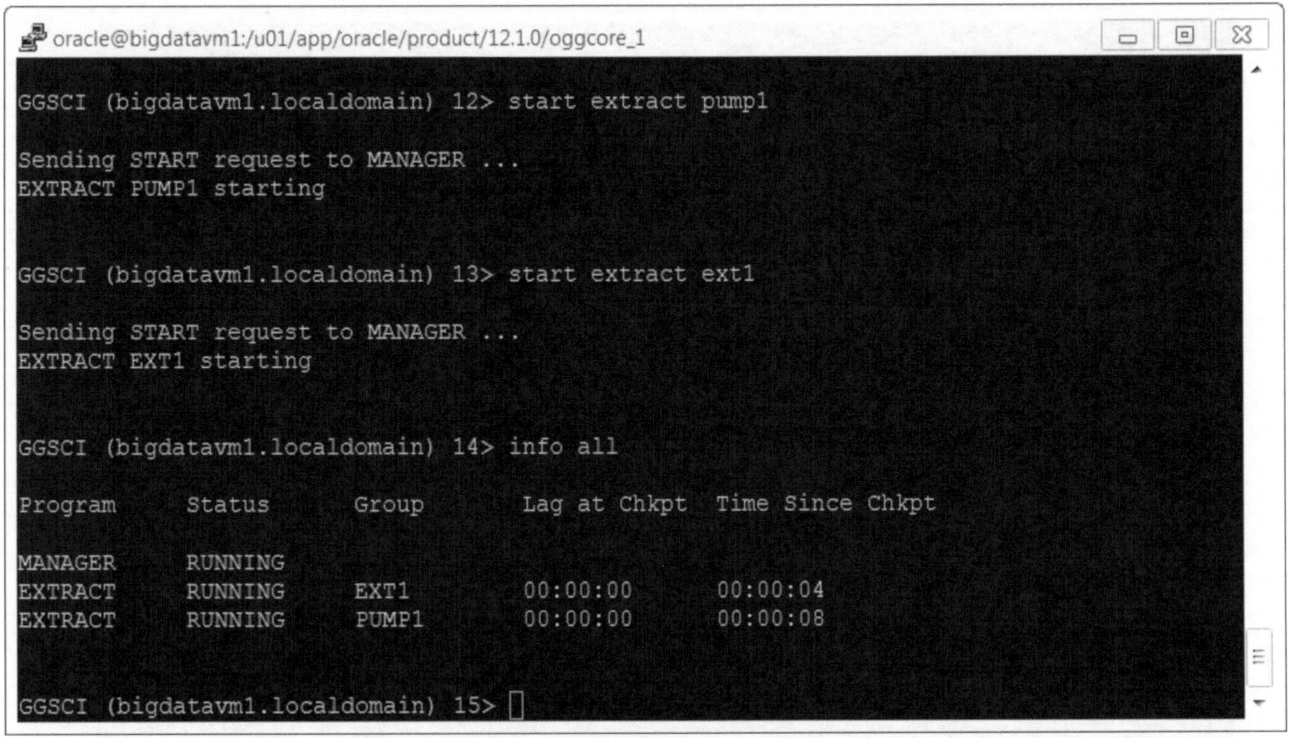

```
oracle@bigdatavm1:/u01/app/oracle/product/12.1.0/oggcore_1

GGSCI (bigdatavml.localdomain) 12> start extract pump1

Sending START request to MANAGER ...
EXTRACT PUMP1 starting

GGSCI (bigdatavml.localdomain) 13> start extract ext1

Sending START request to MANAGER ...
EXTRACT EXT1 starting

GGSCI (bigdatavml.localdomain) 14> info all

Program     Status      Group       Lag at Chkpt  Time Since Chkpt

MANAGER     RUNNING
EXTRACT     RUNNING     EXT1        00:00:00      00:00:04
EXTRACT     RUNNING     PUMP1       00:00:00      00:00:08

GGSCI (bigdatavml.localdomain) 15>
```

Figure 6.13 Starting the Extract and Data Pump Processes on All Three Sources

```
sqlplus facts_events/facts_events@vmdb1
create table test1(id integer);
insert into test1(id) values(801);
commit;
```

and the second source:

```
sqlplus facts_events/facts_events@vmdb2
create table test2(id integer);
insert into test2(id) values(802);
commit;
```

and finally the third source:

```
sqlplus facts_events/facts_events@vmdb3
create table test3(id integer);
insert into test3(id) values(803);
commit;
```

As of the writing of this book, this configuration could not be persuaded to function 100%, where changes were not successfully replicated from any of the three sources to the individual target. The trouble with using Replication to consolidate changes is that those changes must be manually monitored in order to prevent conflicts; correcting and verifying this configuration is beyond the scope of this chapter.

6.5 High Availability with Master-to-Master Replication

Master-to-master replication is generally complicated and often prone to synchronization problems between source and target, because in master-to-master database replication, changes can conflict with each other and must be constantly monitored for and resolved through manual intervention. The other option to high availability, as opposed to master-to-master replication, is clustering of machines that allow multiple machines to share disk space, such as with Oracle RAC or even something like Hadoop and BigData, or even a non-clustered Cloud-based data warehouse like Snowflake or Redshift. The downside to clustering with something like Hadoop or Oracle RAC is that it is usually even more complicated than master-to-master replication. Master-to-master replication can excel where source and target machines are not collocated (right next to each other), making master-to-master replication an effective option to achieve a highly available system that can service customers from more than once source at the same time, presenting a powerful and versatile service to customers, as shown in Figure 6.14.

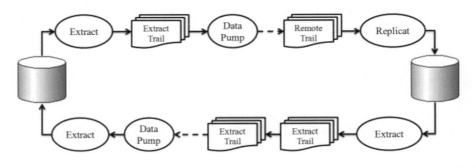

Figure 6.14   Master-to-Master Replication Can Substitute for Non-Colocated Source and Target Servers

6.5.1 Implementing Master-to-Master Replication with GoldenGate

Master-to-master replication always presents problems, regardless of whether we are using GoldenGate or another replication tool. There is some specific functionality that will present problems for master-to-master replication architectures: (1) functions such as TRUNCATE cannot be used because of lack of rollback and logging; (2) keys can have internally generated values, or missing values, or the same values for different data, and might be meaningless to a replicated database; and (3) triggers that generate internal and potentially uncontrollable cascading operations (including the specialized trigger-like function of cascade deletion) can cause generation of disparate data sets between source and target. Database replication is all about synchronization of change between a source and a target, and making changes that go both ways can create tremendous possibility for conflict.

6.6 So What's Next?

This chapter has described and demonstrated some ways in which GoldenGate can be applied as a middleware software layer in order to architect multiple server structures, including live reporting, standby, distribution, data warehousing, and high availability. Not every architectural application is applicable for detailed implementation by example in a book such as this one—being too advanced in some areas; other resources online and in printed form can be used, including GoldenGate documentation from Oracle Corporation. The next chapter will wrap up this book with a number of sections that consolidate useful sequences of action.

Chapter 7

Wrapping It Up

The goal of this chapter is to describe sequences of steps that consolidate a basic deinstall of GoldenGate followed by a basic reinstall of Golden-Gate, in addition to a list of references that were used in the writing of this book.

7.1 Deinstalling GoldenGate

This section describes the sequential steps required in order to deinstall and remove GoldenGate software, as well as changes required to be made to a supporting Oracle® Database.

7.1.1 Stop the GoldenGate Processes

Stop all processes, ending with the manager process on both source and target systems (processes in this case are already removed):

```
cd $ORACLE_GG
ggsci
stop ER *
stop manager
```

and it looks like this below, which is already removed for this case:

```
GGSCI (bigdata.localdomain) 2> stop ER *
No ER groups found, but some coordinated threads may have been
excluded.
```

and the manager process is already stopped:

```
GGSCI (bigdata.localdomain) 3> stop manager
Manager is already stopped.
```

7.1.2 Removing DDL

Execute SQLPLUS on both source and target to remove DDL replication from each database:

```
cd $ORACLE_GG
sqlplus /as sysdba
```

and inside SQLPLUS:

```
@ddl_disable.sql;
@ddl_remove.sql;
@marker_remove.sql;
```

7.1.3 Removing Objects

Now go back into GGSCI to remove table- and schema-level supplemental logging from source and target—but given the later dropping of the GGATE tablespace and user, this step is not strictly necessary; however, including this information here helps in understanding the separate steps:

```
cd $ORACLE_GG
ggsci
DBLOGIN USERID ggate
DELETE TRANDATA dmevents.earthquake
DELETE TRANDATA dmevents.volcano
DELETE SCHEMATRANDATA email
DELETE SCHEMATRANDATA bigdata
```

   And now remove the Extract process on the source:

```
DELETE EXTRACT ext1
UNREGISTER EXTRACT ext1 DATABASE
```

and the Replicat process on the target:

```
DELETE REPLICAT rep1
UNREGISTER REPLICAT rep1 DATABASE
```

7.1.4 Uninstalling Oracle GoldenGate

Find the path of GoldenGate and execute the deinstall.sh script using the full path name on both servers:

```
/u01/app/oracle/product/12.1.0/oggcore_1/deinstall/deinstall.sh
```

   The result should look something like this:

```
/u01/app/oracle/product/12.1.0/oggcore_1/deinstall/deinstall.sh

ALERT: Ensure all the processes running from the current
Oracle Home are shutdown prior to running this software
uninstallation script.
```

```
Proceed with removing Oracle GoldenGate home: /u01/app/oracle/
product/12.1.0/oggcore_1 (yes/no)? [no]
yes
Starting Oracle Universal Installer...

Checking swap space: must be greater than 500 MB.    Actual
8197 MB     Passed
Preparing to launch Oracle Universal Installer from /tmp/
OraInstall2017-01-24_12
-32-59AM. Please wait ...Oracle Universal Installer, Version
11.2.0.3.0 Production
Copyright (C) 1999, 2011, Oracle. All rights reserved.

Starting deinstall

Deinstall in progress (Tuesday, January 24, 2017 12:33:10 AM EST)
.................................................. 100% Done.

Deinstall successful

End of install phases.(Tuesday, January 24, 2017 12:33:34 AM EST)
End of deinstallations
Please check '/u01/app/oraInventory/logs/silentInstall2017-01-
24_12-32-59AM.log' for more details.
```

7.1.5 Removing GGATE User and Tablespace in Oracle Database

It might be necessary to restart a database before removing the GGATE user:

```
DROP USER ggate CASCADE;
DROP TABLESPACE ggate INCLUDING CONTENTS AND DATAFILES;
```

7.2 Reinstalling GoldenGate

This section describes the sequential steps of reinstalling GoldenGate software onto a clean system.

7.2.1 Restart Oracle Databases

Forcibly restart to help clear any leftover connected processes:

```
sqlplus / as sysdba
shutdown immediate;
startup;
```

7.2.2 Recreate Tablespace

Recreate the GGATE tablespace on both source and target servers, starting on the source:

```
sqlplus / as sysdba
CREATE BIGFILE TABLESPACE ggate
      DATAFILE '/u02/app/oracle/oradata/bigdata/ggate01.dbf'
SIZE 1G AUTOEXTEND ON;
CREATE USER ggate IDENTIFIED BY ggate
      DEFAULT TABLESPACE ggate TEMPORARY TABLESPACE TEMP;
GRANT DBA, CONNECT, RESOURCE, UNLIMITED TABLESPACE TO ggate;
GRANT EXECUTE ON UTL_FILE TO ggate;
GRANT FLASHBACK ANY TABLE TO ggate;
```

and on the target:

```
CREATE BIGFILE TABLESPACE ggate
      DATAFILE '/u02/app/oracle/oradata/failover/ggate01.dbf'
      SIZE 1G AUTOEXTEND ON;
CREATE USER ggate IDENTIFIED BY ggate
      DEFAULT TABLESPACE ggate TEMPORARY TABLESPACE TEMP;
GRANT DBA, CONNECT, RESOURCE, UNLIMITED TABLESPACE TO ggate;
GRANT EXECUTE ON UTL_FILE TO ggate;
GRANT FLASHBACK ANY TABLE TO ggate;
```

7.2.3 Reinstall GoldenGate Software

Rebuild GoldenGate software on both source and target, starting with VNC, following the instructions at the following URL:

```
http://www.oracletroubleshooter.com/using-vncserver
```

If VNC is not running:

```
[root@bigdata ~]# ps -ef | grep vnc
root       7554  4247  0 11:40 pts/1     00:00:00 grep vnc
[root@bigdata ~]#
```

reset the VNC password by removing the password file and recreating it on both source and target:

```
[root@bigdata ~]# ls /root/.vnc
bigdata.localdomain:1.log  bigdata.localdomain:1.pid  bigdata.
localdomain:2.log  bigdata.localdomain:2.pid  passwd  xstartup
[root@bigdata ~]# rm /root/.vnc/passwd
rm: remove regular file '/root/.vnc/passwd'? y
[root@bigdata ~]# vncserver

You will require a password to access your desktops.

Password:
Verify:

New 'bigdata.localdomain:1 (root)' desktop is bigdata.
localdomain:1

Starting applications specified in /root/.vnc/xstartup
Log file is /root/.vnc/bigdata.localdomain:1.log
```

Connect to the oracle Linux user on both source and target, download (see Chapter 2) and unzip the GoldenGate software if needed:

```
su - oracle
cd /oinstall
unzip fbo_ggs_Linux_x64_shiphome.zip
```

Use TightVNC (see Chapter 2 for TightVNC installation) to emulate source and target server screens to a client machine, as shown in Figure 7.1.

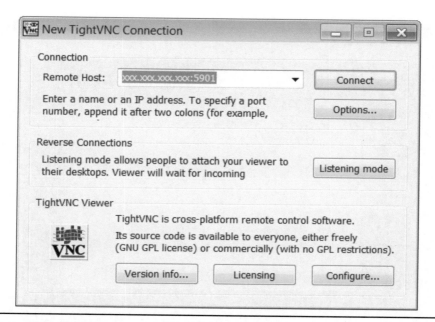

Figure 7.1   Emulate a Server on a Client Machine

Connect to the server using the VNC password added when executing vncserver in the operating system, on both the source and target servers, as shown in Figure 7.2.

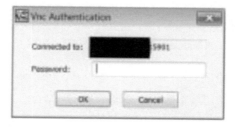

Figure 7.2   Connect to a Server Using VNC and TightVNC

Open up an xterm terminal Window in the X terminal emulation on the Linux server, redirect the host DISPLAY, and connect to the oracle Linux user, as shown in Figure 7.3.

And this is the current .bash_profile for the oracle Linux user, as shown in Figure 7.4.

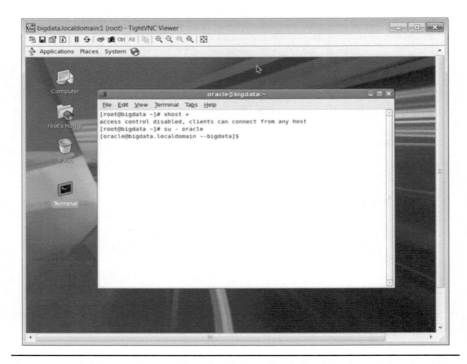

Figure 7.3   Starting an xterm in TightVNC to Emulate Linux X to a Client Machine

```
                              oracle@bigdata:~                          _ □ ×
 File  Edit  View  Terminal  Tabs  Help ▶
 [oracle@bigdata.localdomain ~-bigdata]$ cat .bash_profile |more
 if [ -f ~/.bashrc ]; then
         . ~/.bashrc
 fi

 umask 022

 export PATH=$PATH:$HOME/bin:/bin:/usr/bin:/usr/local/bin:/etc:..:/usr/sbin

 export ORACLE_BASE=/u01/app/oracle
 export ORACLE_HOME=$ORACLE_BASE/product/12.1.0/dbhome_1
 export ORACLE_GG=$ORACLE_BASE/product/12.1.0/oggcore_1
 export ORACLE_SID=bigdata
 export LD_LIBRARY_PATH=$ORACLE_HOME/lib
 export LD_LIBRARY_PATH=$LD_LIBRARY_PATH:$ORACLE_GG
 export TNS_ADMIN=$ORACLE_HOME/network/admin
 export TRACE=$ORACLE_BASE/diag/rdbms/$ORACLE_SID/$ORACLE_SID/trace
 export PATH=$PATH:$ORACLE_BASE:$ORACLE_HOME:$ORACLE_HOME/bin:$TNS_ADMIN:$ORACLE_HOME/OPatch
 export PATH=$PATH:$ORACLE_GG
 export TMP=/tmp
 export BACKUPS=/u02/app/oracle/backups
 export SCRIPT_HOST=`hostname -s`

 PS1="[\u@\H \W-`echo $ORACLE_SID`]\$ "

 export HOST=`hostname -s`
```

Figure 7.4   The Oracle Linux user .bash_profile for Oracle Database and GoldenGate

And these are the aliases currently in use on my servers inside my oracle Linux user .bash_profile file:

```
[oracle@bigdata.localdomain ~-bigdata]$ alias
alias alert='cd $TRACE'
alias backups='cd $BACKUPS'
alias base='cd $ORACLE_BASE'
alias dbs='cd $ORACLE_HOME/dbs'
alias dbstart='. $HOME/scripts/dbstart.sh'
alias dbstop='. $HOME/scripts/dbstop.sh'
alias gghome='cd $ORACLE_GG'
alias ggsci='gghome; ggsci'
alias home='cd $ORACLE_HOME'
alias l.='ls -d .* --color=tty'
alias ll='ls -l --color=tty'
alias ls='ls --color=tty'
alias lsnrlog='cd $ORACLE_BASE/diag/tnslsnr/$HOST/listener/trace'
alias rm='rm -i'
alias scripts='cd $HOME/scripts'
alias sqlnetlog='cd $ORACLE_HOME/network/log'
alias sqlnettrc='cd $ORACLE_HOME/network/trace'
alias startgg='gghome; echo obey "start" | ./ggsci'
alias stopgg='gghome; echo obey "stop" | ./ggsci'
alias tns='cd $TNS_ADMIN'
alias vi='vim'
alias which='alias | /usr/bin/which --tty-only --read-alias
--show-dot --show-tilde'
```

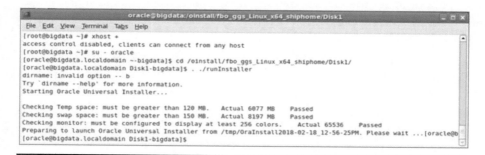

Figure 7.5   Running the Runinstaller Script

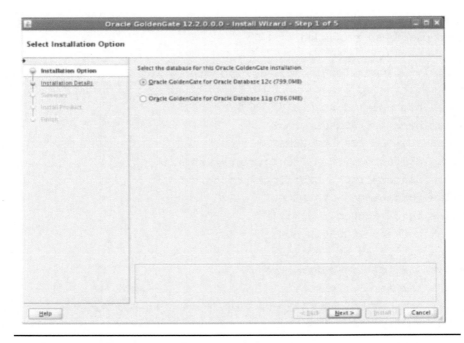

Figure 7.6 GoldenGate Installation Screen 1

Now we can install GoldenGate software inside the TightVNC X emulator shown on the screens in sequence, as shown by the following and in Figure 7.5 and Figure 7.6.

```
cd /oinstall/fbo_ggs_Linux_x64_shiphome/Disk1
. runInstaller
```

Be sure to set the GoldenGate home to the correct path as highlighted in Figure 7.7 where the default might include the Oracle Database software home, which is incorrect.

Click the highlighted Install button when ready as shown in Figure 7.8, Figure 7.9, and Figure 7.10.

Don't forget to execute the GoldenGate installation process on both source and target servers.

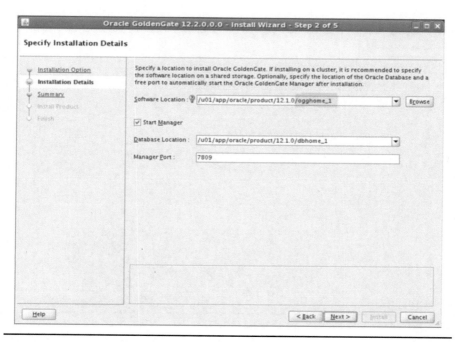

Figure 7.7   GoldenGate Installation Screen 2

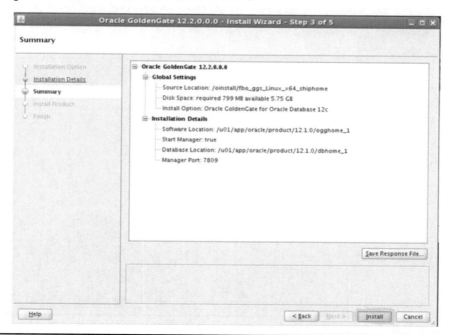

Figure 7.8   GoldenGate Installation Screen 3

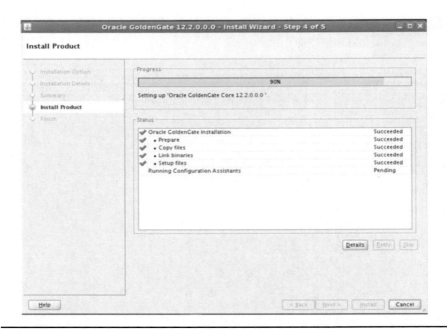

Figure 7.9   GoldenGate Installation Screen 4

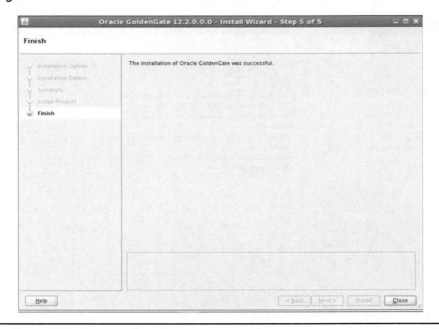

Figure 7.10   GoldenGate Installation Screen 5

7.2.4 Database-Level Logging and Configuration

Check and implement on both source and target if improperly set, beginning with checking that archive log mode is set:

```
sqlplus / as sysdba
ARCHIVE LOG LIST;
```

If the result shown is no archive log mode:

```
SHUTDOWN IMMEDIATE;
STARTUP MOUNT;
ALTER DATABASE ARCHIVELOG;
ALTER DATABASE OPEN;
```

supplemental logging must be configured on the source and target (assuming future standby reversal):

```
ALTER DATABASE ADD SUPPLEMENTAL LOG DATA;
ALTER DATABASE FORCE LOGGING;
```

Increase undo retention size on the source only to account for flashback:

```
ALTER SYSTEM SET UNDO_RETENTION=86400 SCOPE=BOTH;
```

Set the STREAMS_POOL_SIZE parameter on the source only:

```
ALTER SYSTEM SET STREAMS_POOL_SIZE=1280M SCOPE=BOTH;
```

Oracle12c requires a parameter on both source and target to enable GoldenGate:

```
ALTER SYSTEM SET enable_goldengate_replication=true
SCOPE=both;
```

7.2.5 Schema-Level Application Logging

Apply schema-level logging to non-Oracle application schemas on the source; below are databases in my database:

```
cd $ORACLE_GG
ggsci
DBLOGIN USERID ggate, PASSWORD ggate
ADD SCHEMATRANDATA dimensions
ADD SCHEMATRANDATA email
ADD SCHEMATRANDATA facts
ADD SCHEMATRANDATA facts_events
ADD SCHEMATRANDATA finance
```

7.2.6 Supporting DDL Replication

Run these commands on the source only, adding in the GGATE schema name where prompted:

```
cd $ORACLE_GG
sqlplus / as sysdba
@marker_setup.sql
@ddl_setup.sql
@role_setup.sql
grant GGS_GGSUSER_ROLE to ggate;
@ddl_enable.sql
```

7.2.7 Extraction and Application Users

Create users on the source only:

```
create user capture identified by capture default tablespace
users temporary tablespace temp;
grant connect,resource,unlimited tablespace to capture;

create user appli identified by appli default tablespace users
temporary tablespace temp;
grant connect,resource,unlimited tablespace to appli;
```

7.2.8 Configure and Start the Source

Create subdirs on both source and target, and start the manager process if it's not yet started:

```
ggsci
create subdirs
info all
START MANAGER
```

Create the Extract process on the source, the extract trail on the source, link it into the Extract process, and finally edit (create) the extract parameters on the source:

```
ADD EXTRACT ext1, TRANLOG, BEGIN NOW
ADD EXTTRAIL /u01/app/oracle/product/12.1.0/oggcore_1/dirdat/
lt, EXTRACT ext1
EDIT PARAMS ext1
```

This is the content of the ext1 extract parameters file on the source:

```
EXTRACT ext1
USERID ggate, password ggate
rmthost failover, mgrport 7809
rmttrail /u01/app/oracle/product/12.1.0/oggcore_1/dirdat/lt
--This supports collection of DDL from the CAPTURE schema
ddl include mapped objname capture.*
--This supports collection of DML from the CAPTURE schema
table capture.*;
```

Create the checkpoint table on the target in the global parameters file:

```
ggsci
EDIT PARAMS ./GLOBAL
```

And add these lines to the ./GLOBAL parameters file:

```
GGSCHEMA ggate
CHECKPOINTTABLE ggate.CHECKPOINT
```

Connect as the GGATE user in GGSCI:

```
DBLOGIN USERID ggate, PASSWORD ggate
ADD CHECKPOINTTABLE ggate.CHECKPOINT
```

Add the Replicat group on the target and link between the extract trail and the checkpoint table:

```
ADD REPLICAT rep1, EXTTRAIL /u01/app/oracle/product/12.1.0/
oggcore_1/dirdat/lt, CHECKPOINTTABLE ggate.CHECKPOINT
```

Edit the Replicat parameters file on the target:

```
EDIT PARAMS rep1
```

Add this to the Replicat parameter file on the target:

```
REPLICAT rep1
ASSUMETARGETDEFS
USERID ggate, PASSWORD ggate
DISCARDFILE /u01/app/oracle/product/12.1.0/oggcore_1/dirdat/
rep1_discard.txt, APPEND, MEGABYTES 10
--Maps tables from source to target
MAP CAPTURE.*, TARGET APPLI.*;
```

Now check the manager process parameters on both source and target:

```
edit params mgr
```

This should be in the file as defined above for the RMTHOST setting:

```
PORT 7809
```

Start the Extract process on the source:

```
START EXTRACT ext1
```

INFO ALL on the source should look like this:

```
GGSCI (bigdata.localdomain) 15> info all
Program     Status     Group     Lag at Chkpt   Time Since Chkpt
MANAGER     RUNNING
EXTRACT     RUNNING    EXT1      00:00:00       00:33:50
```

Start the Replicat process on the target:

```
START REPLICAT rep1
```

INFO ALL on the target should look like this:

```
GGSCI (failover.localdomain as ggate@failover) 20> info all
Program      Status      Group      Lag at Chkpt   Time Since Chkpt
MANAGER      RUNNING
REPLICAT     RUNNING     REP1       00:00:00       00:00:00
```

Registration of EXTRACT and REPLICAT processes are not needed here because Integrated Apply is not in use in this configuration.

If there were any errors then alter the Extract or Replicat process position to after the change and restart it as follows:

```
STOP EXTRACT ext1
ALTER EXTRACT ext1, BEGIN NOW
START EXTRACT ext1
```

or:

```
STOP REPLICAT rep1
ALTER EXTRACT rep1, BEGIN NOW
START EXTRACT rep1
```

7.2.9 Test Replication

Create a table on the source, add some rows and select replicated data at the target:

```
sqlplus / as sysdba
CONNECT capture/capture@bigdata
CREATE TABLE test(id INTEGER PRIMARY KEY);
INSERT INTO test(id) VALUES(1);
COMMIT;
```

On the target (it could take a few minutes to replicate):

```
sqlplus appli/appli@failover

SQL*Plus: Release 12.1.0.2.0 Production on Tue Mar 14 15:03:06
2017
Copyright (c) 1982, 2014, Oracle.  All rights reserved.
Last Successful login time: Tue Mar 14 2017 15:02:45 -04:00
Connected to:
Oracle Database 12c Enterprise Edition Release 12.1.0.2.0 -
64bit Production
With the Partitioning, OLAP, Advanced Analytics and Real
Application Testing options

SQL> select * from test;
        ID
----------
         1
```

7.2.10 Add New Schemas

New schemas in the database are added in the EXTRACT parameters file:

```
EXTRACT ext1
USERID ggate, password ggate
rmthost failover, mgrport 7809
rmttrail /u01/app/oracle/product/12.1.0/oggcore_1/dirdat/lt
ddl include mapped objname capture.*, include mapped objname
dimensions.*, include mapped objname email.*, include mapped
objname facts.* , include mapped objname facts_events.* ,
include mapped objname finance.*
table DIMENSIONS.*;
table EMAIL.*;
table FACTS.*;
table FACTS_EVENTS.*;
table FINANCE.*;
```

And the REPLICAT parameters on the target:

```
REPLICAT rep1
```

```
ASSUMETARGETDEFS
USERID ggate, PASSWORD ggate
DISCARDFILE /u01/app/oracle/product/12.1.0/oggcore_1/dirdat/
repl_discard.txt, APPEND, MEGABYTES 10
DDL
--Maps tables from source to target
MAP CAPTURE.*, TARGET APPLI.*;
MAP DIMENSIONS.*, TARGET DIMENSIONS.*;
MAP EMAIL.*, TARGET EMAIL.*;
MAP FACTS.*, TARGET FACTS.*;
MAP FACTS_EVENTS.*, TARGET FACTS_EVENTS.*;
MAP FINANCE.*, TARGET FINANCE.*;
```

Stop and start the manager and Extract process on the source, plus the manager and Replicat processes on the target, and test:

```
sqlplus dimensions/dimensions@bigdata
CREATE TABLE test(id INTEGER PRIMARY KEY);
INSERT INTO test(id) VALUES(1);
INSERT INTO test(id) VALUES(2);
INSERT INTO test(id) VALUES(3);
COMMIT;

CONNECT email/email@bigdata
CREATE TABLE test(id INTEGER PRIMARY KEY);
INSERT INTO test(id) VALUES(1);
INSERT INTO test(id) VALUES(2);
INSERT INTO test(id) VALUES(3);
COMMIT;
```

And verify replication on the target:

```
[oracle@failover.localdomain ~-failover]$ sqlplus / as sysdba

SQL*Plus: Release 12.1.0.2.0 Production on Tue Feb 20 01:53:58
2018

Copyright (c) 1982, 2014, Oracle.  All rights reserved.
```

```
Connected to:
Oracle Database 12c Enterprise Edition Release 12.1.0.2.0 -
64bit Production
With the Partitioning, OLAP, Advanced Analytics and Real
Application Testing options

SQL> select * from dimensions.test;

        ID
----------
         1
         2
         3

SQL> select * from email.test;

        ID
----------
         1
         2
         3

SQL>
```

7.2.11 Script Only Basic Replication

This additional section is a script included as a recently tested example of a sequence that creates a replicated schema called GPOWELL, built with a clean install of a new Oracle database on source and target, plus removing and reinstalling GoldenGate completely:

```
--source
sqlplus / as sysdba
CREATE BIGFILE TABLESPACE ggate DATAFILE '/u01/app/oracle/
oradata/vmdb1/ggate01.dbf' SIZE 1G AUTOEXTEND ON;
CREATE USER ggate IDENTIFIED BY ggate DEFAULT TABLESPACE ggate
TEMPORARY TABLESPACE TEMP;
GRANT DBA, CONNECT, RESOURCE, UNLIMITED TABLESPACE TO ggate;
```

```
GRANT EXECUTE ON UTL_FILE TO ggate;
GRANT FLASHBACK ANY TABLE TO ggate;

--target
CREATE BIGFILE TABLESPACE ggate DATAFILE '/u01/app/oracle/
oradata/vmdb2/ggate01.dbf' SIZE 1G AUTOEXTEND ON;
CREATE USER ggate IDENTIFIED BY ggate
DEFAULT TABLESPACE ggate TEMPORARY TABLESPACE TEMP;
GRANT DBA, CONNECT, RESOURCE, UNLIMITED TABLESPACE TO ggate;
GRANT EXECUTE ON UTL_FILE TO ggate;
GRANT FLASHBACK ANY TABLE TO ggate;

-source & target
create user gpowell identified by gpowell;
grant connect,resource,dba to gpowell;
grant select any dictionary to gpowell;
grant select_catalog_role to gpowell;
grant unlimited tablespace to gpowell;

--source (& target for standby reversal)
add schematrandata gpowell

--source (& target for standby reversal)
@marker_setup.sql
@ddl_setup.sql
@role_setup.sql
grant GGS_GGSUSER_ROLE to ggate;
@ddl_enable.sql
ALTER DATABASE ADD SUPPLEMENTAL LOG DATA;
ALTER DATABASE FORCE LOGGING;

--source & target
create subdirs

--source
ADD EXTRACT ext1, TRANLOG, BEGIN NOW
ADD EXTTRAIL /u01/app/oracle/product/12.1.0/oggcore_1/dirdat/
lt, EXTRACT ext1
```

```
--why not add equivalent RMTTRAIL as well???

--source
edit params ext1

EXTRACT ext1
USERID ggate, password ggate
rmthost bigdatavm2, mgrport 7809
rmttrail /u01/app/oracle/product/12.1.0/oggcore_1/dirdat/lt
ddl include mapped objname gpowell.*
table gpowell.*;

--target
EDIT PARAMS ./GLOBAL

GGSCHEMA ggate
CHECKPOINTTABLE ggate.CHECKPOINT

DBLOGIN USERID ggate, PASSWORD ggate
ADD CHECKPOINTTABLE ggate.CHECKPOINT

--target
ADD REPLICAT rep1, EXTTRAIL /u01/app/oracle/product/12.1.0/
oggcore_1/dirdat/lt, CHECKPOINTTABLE ggate.CHECKPOINT

--target
EDIT PARAMS rep1

--target
REPLICAT rep1
ASSUMETARGETDEFS
USERID ggate, PASSWORD ggate
DISCARDFILE /u01/app/oracle/product/12.1.0/oggcore_1/dirdat/
rep1_discard.txt, APPEND, MEGABYTES 10
MAP GPOWELL.*, TARGET GPOWELL.*;

--define the replicat process
```

```
REPLICAT rep1
--connect as a DDL supporting database user
USERID ggate, PASSWORD ggate
ASSUMETARGETDEFS
--source and target databases use the same schema names in
this case
MAP bigdata.*, TARGET bigdata.*;

--in case of error reset
ALTER EXTRACT ext1, BEGIN NOW
ALTER REPLICAT rep1, BEGIN NOW
```

7.2.12 GoldenGate Silent Installations

A silent GoldenGate installation is useful when something like VNC cannot be used to emulate Linux to another machine away from the server, such as me on my laptop. This is how it is done:

```
cd /oinstall/fb...

./runInstaller -silent -responseFile /oinstall/fbo_ggs_Linux_
x64_shiphome/Disk1/oggcore.rsp
```

This is the response file content using a cat command:

```
cat oggcore.rsp

################################################################
## Copyright(c) Oracle Corporation 2014. All rights reserved.##
##                                                           ##
## Specify values for the variables listed below to          ##
## customize your installation.                              ##
##                                                           ##
## Each variable is associated with a comment. The comment   ##
## can help to populate the variables with the appropriate   ##
## values.                                                    ##
##                                                           ##
```

```
## IMPORTANT NOTE: This file should be secured to have read ##
## permission only by the oracle user or an administrator   ##
## who own this installation to protect any sensitive input ##
## values.                                                   ##
################################################################

#--------------------------------------------------------------
# Do not change the following system generated value.
#--------------------------------------------------------------
oracle.install.responseFileVersion=/oracle/install/
rspfmt_ogginstall_response_schema_v12_1_2

################################################################
##                                                          ##
## Oracle GoldenGate installation option and details        ##
##                                                          ##
################################################################

#--------------------------------------------------------------
# Specify the installation option.
# Specify ORA12c for installing Oracle GoldenGate for Oracle
          Database 12c and
#         ORA11g for installing Oracle GoldenGate for Oracle
          Database 11g
#--------------------------------------------------------------
INSTALL_OPTION=ORA12c

#--------------------------------------------------------------
# Specify a location to install Oracle GoldenGate
#--------------------------------------------------------------
SOFTWARE_LOCATION=/u01/app/oracle/product/12.1.0/oggcore_1

#--------------------------------------------------------------
# Specify true to start the manager after installation.
#--------------------------------------------------------------
START_MANAGER=
```

```
#---------------------------------------------------------------
# Specify a free port within the valid range for the manager
  process.
# Required only if START_MANAGER is true.
#---------------------------------------------------------------
MANAGER_PORT=


#---------------------------------------------------------------
# Specify the location of the Oracle Database.
# Required only if START_MANAGER is true.
#---------------------------------------------------------------
DATABASE_LOCATION=/u01/app/oracle/product/12.1.0/dbhome_1


###############################################################
##                                                         ##
## Specify details to Create inventory for Oracle installs  ##
##                                                         ##
## Required only for the first Oracle product install on a  ##
## system.                                                 ##
##                                                         ##
###############################################################


#---------------------------------------------------------------
# Specify the location which holds the install inventory files.
# This is an optional parameter if installing on
# Windows based Operating System.
#---------------------------------------------------------------
INVENTORY_LOCATION=/u01/app/oraInventory


#---------------------------------------------------------------
# Unix group to be set for the inventory directory.
# This parameter is not applicable if installing on
# Windows based Operating System.
#---------------------------------------------------------------
UNIX_GROUP_NAME=oinstall
```

7.3 References

Numerous references were used in this book including use of Oracle documentation as well as other online references, starting with Oracle GoldenGate documentation online:

```
https://docs.oracle.com/goldengate/c1221/gg-winux/index.html
```

And other online references:

```
blog.moserit.com/how-to-centrally-manage-encrypted-goldengate-
passwords-with-macros
blogs.oracle.com/imc/entry/
oracle_goldengate_configuring_ddl_replication
docs.oracle.com/goldengate/1212/gg-winux/GIORA/additional_
config.htm#GIORA376
docs.oracle.com/goldengate/1212/gg-winux/GIORA/ddl.
htm#GIORA959
docs.oracle.com/goldengate/1212/gg-winux/GIORA/setup.
htm#GIORA37
docs.oracle.com/goldengate/1212/gg-winux/GIORA/setup.
htm#GIORA374
docs.oracle.com/goldengate/1212/gg-winux/GIORA/system_
requirements.htm
docs.oracle.com/goldengate/1212/gg-winux/GIORA/system_
requirements.htm#GIORA122
docs.oracle.com/goldengate/1212/gg-winux/GWUAD/wu_security.
htm#GWUAD354
docs.oracle.com/goldengate/1212/gg-winux/GWURF/ggsci_commands.
htm#GWURF110
docs.oracle.com/goldengate/c1221/gg-winux/GWURF/summary-
oracle-goldengate-parameters.htm#GWURF978
http:/docs.oracle.com/goldengate/c1221/gg-winux/GWURF/summary-
oracle-goldengate-commands.htm
jinyuwang.weebly.com/core-platform/
oracle-goldengate-globalization
minersoracleblog.wordpress.com/2013/05/23/
oracle-goldengate-initial-load-techniques/
```

```
practical-tech.blogspot.com/2012/03/oracle-goldengate-basic-
dml-replication.html
sachinichake.wordpress.com/2013/05/08/
step-by-step-golden-gate-configuration/
www.dba-oracle.com/t_goldengate_data_loading_overview.htm
www.juliandyke.com/Research/GoldenGate/
GoldenGateBasicConfiguration.php
www.oracle.com
www.oracle.com/technetwork/middleware/ias/downloads/fusion-
certification-100350.html
www.oracle-scn.com/oracle-goldengate-initial-load-file-to-
database-utility-method/
www.oracletroubleshooter.com/using-vncserver
www.pythian.com/blog/oracle-goldengate-installation-part-1/
```

7.4 The End

During the process of building the chapters in this book, I found it very useful to utilize the consolidated deinstallation and reinstallation sequences of events presented in this chapter, so to me it only makes sense that you the reader would also find these sections useful. The references are also useful and can help with specifics as well as further reading if you decide to dig into the much more detailed aspects of Oracle GoldenGate replication software.

Glossary

alias	A simpler substitute command for a more complex command
apply	The process that describes how change is applied to a target database
automated switchover	Where a standby database primary fails and automatically switches all activity to a secondary failover server, the automated form of which is not available in GoldenGate
bi-directional replication	*See* master to master
BigData	A database architecture that allows for very large data structure by use of clustered mirrors containing duplicate datasets, which do not necessarily maintain consistency between copies
bigdata database	Used to store very large amounts of data, allows constant change, but also allows for very large scale and analytics and reporting; examples are the Hadoop framework, MongoDB, Google's BigQuery, Facebook's Casandra
broadcast replication	*See* distribution

capture	The process that describes how change is captured on a source database
cascading replication	Hierarchical form of replication where chain of databases replicate from source to target, and then from target to another target, and so on
checkpoint	A frozen position in time storing the state of a database and its changes at a specified time
cold copying	Generally implies that all software that can make changes to a database is shut down during a copying process
commit	A SQL command that forces changes to be made permanent in a relational database
commit sequence number (CSN)	A sequence number used to track changes replicated by GoldenGate
consolidation replication	See data warehouse
credentials store	Used in GoldenGate to store credentials, such as username and password, for a more automated and seamless connection to a GoldenGate installation
data	The content stored in tables (see metadata)
data consolidation	A process of replicating and consolidating data from more than one source server in a single target server, such as for a data warehouse target database
Data Definition Language (DDL)	The database language used to change objects in a database
data distribution	A process of replicating and sharing data from one source to multiple targets
Data Manipulation Language (DML)	The database language used to change data in a database

data warehouse	Specialized write append and read only data for very large amounts of data
database-level supplemental logging	Adds extra information to Oracle Database redo log files for everything in database
Data Pump	An Oracle utility that moves data efficiently from one place to another, both on the same server, between servers, and even between databases
datatype, data type	A mapping mechanism that forces data values to be formatted in a specified manner
deinstall	*See* uninstall
Extract process	The GoldenGate process that executes the replication process on the source (see source database)
extract trail	A file that records change made on a source, which will be transferred and applied to a target database
extract, transport, and load (ETL)	Extract from a source database, transport to a target database server, and load into a target database; can also include transformation or changes to data
failover, failover database	*See* standby database
flashback	Allows for a table to be viewed at a previous point in time, in a previous state before changes were made after the flashpoint juncture
GGSCI history	A history of commands submitted in the GGSCI tool on a GoldenGate server installation
globalized character set	Flexibility with many languages including any script
GoldenGate	Software owned by Oracle Corporation used for database replication between many different database vendors

GoldenGate config- uration parameters	Parameter files used to control the configuration and behavior of GoldenGate processes
GoldenGate Software Command Line Interface (GGSCI)	A shell command line tool for managing and administering Oracle GoldenGate replication middleware
grouping	Used to describe a set of a single type of process, which can execute the same type of process in parallel on the same server
high-availability databases	Generally this type of database architecture utilizes multiple servers to allow for instant access to a database if one database in a group of replicated databases fails; continuity of service is possible with master-to-master replication
hot copying	Copying an Oracle database with all database software online, while still allowing changes to be made to that database at the same time
Integrated Apply	A configuration method for application of change to a target database
Integrated Capture	A configuration method for capture of change from a source database
Linux®	An open source operating system that places UNIX®-like software on a much cheaper Intel platform
live reporting	Describes how reporting is produced in real time for customer and consumer consumption of both data as well as meaning of data, presented in both character-based and visually appealing format
Logminer	A process that selects and retrieves specified data items from log files (redo logs in the case of Oracle Database)

Manager process	Manages the basic automated aspects of processing in a GoldenGate installation
master to master	Two databases that copy changes to another database, effectively copying their changes to the other
master to slave	One database copies its changes to another, and the target database does not change (or does not replicat back)
metadata	The data about the data
MySQL	An open source relational database that is owned by Oracle Corporation
OBEY command	Allows for the consolidation and automated execution of multiple GoldenGate commands
online transaction processing (OLTP)	Applies to a type of database that executes many small memory-intensive data change and data-sharing operations concurrently
Oracle Database	Oracle Corporation's flagship product (for now)
Oracle Streams	An Oracle proprietary piece of software that pushes data through a piping process to another Oracle database
Oracle Universal Installer	An installer software used for Oracle software, including Oracle Database
password encryption	Passwords can be encrypted so that unwelcome persons cannot obtain them and steal data
peer-to-peer replication	Master to master, but can include more than two databases
reinstall	A process of rebuilding an Oracle GoldenGate installation on both source and target servers
relational database	Used for processing of highly concurrent, memory-intensive, frequent-change database storage requirements

remote trail	Log files of changes made to a source, transferred to a target database, and to be applied to that target database
Replicat process	The GoldenGate process that executes the replication process on the target (see target database)
replication	The process of automatically copying changes to data from one database to another in order to duplicate database changes in real time to a separate database
reporting	The act of reading data from a database to present a useful presentation or visualization of data to a technical end user or customer
rollback	Undoes any not-yet-commited changes for a session
source database	In replication, the database in which change originates
sql*loader	An Oracle proprietary utility used for loading data into an Oracle database at very high speed
sqlplus	An Oracle proprietary SQL coding and submission utility
standby, standby database	Intended for automated switching from an active database to a copy when the primary database develops a problem; can also be used for maintenance, but that is not its principal purpose
Structured Query Language (SQL)	An ANSII standard declarative programming language used to retrieve data from a relational database such as Oracle Database
system change number (SCN)	A change vector used by Oracle Database to locate a database change state across multiple Oracle Database files
table-level supplemental logging	Adds extra information to Oracle Database redo log files for individually specified tables

target database	In replication the database where change is replicated to
trail	A file containing a record of changes to a database, which can be used to replicate change to another database
Transparent Network Substrate (TNS)	Oracle proprietary networking software for Oracle software
unidirectional replication	*See* master-to-master replication
uninstall	A process of removing software from a server, in this case GoldenGate software and associated configuration with source and target Oracle databases
UNIX	*See* Linux
VIEW SSGEVT	A GoldenGate tool used to examine GoldenGate logging, particularly when searching for causes of error conditions
Virtual Network Computing (VNC)	A tool that allows for emulation of a graphical operating system to a remote screen, in the next room or across the world
Windows® operating system	The popular operating system produced by Microsoft® Corporation

Index